10 INDIAN TRIBES

AND THE UNIQUE LIVES THEY LEAD

NIDHI DUGAR KUNDALIA

Read more in the 10s series

10 INDIAN TRIBES AND THE UNIQUE LIVES THEY LEAD

NIDHI DUGAR KUNDALIA

duckbill

An imprint of Penguin Random House

PENGUIN BOOKS

USA | Canada | UK | Ireland | Australia
New Zealand | India | South Africa | China

Duckbill Books is part of the Penguin Random House group of companies
whose addresses can be found at global.penguinrandomhouse.com

Published by Penguin Random House India Pvt. Ltd
4th Floor, Capital Tower 1, MG Road,
Gurugram 122 002, Haryana, India

Penguin
Random House
India

First published in Duckbill Books by
Penguin Random House India 2023

ISBN 9780143453154

Typeset in Sitka by DiTech Publishing Services Pvt. Ltd
Printed at Replika Press Pvt. Ltd, India

www.penguin.co.in

MIX
Paper from
responsible sources
FSC® C016779

10

INTRODUCTION

Centuries have passed since anthropologists first started trying to define what a tribe is. And even today, there is no complete agreement on the definition. Each definition seems to vary, depending upon field situation, as witnessed by those proposing the definition. You may have thought of song, costumes and dance when you picked this book. Whether you call them Adivasi (first inhabitants), janjati (forest dwellers) or scheduled tribes—who really are tribal peoples beyond the colour that are depicted in media and popular imagination?

While researching the ten tribes in the book, I found a commonality among them all. Each tribe shared a territorial association, was united in language and recognized social distance from other communities.

The word 'Adivasi' was coined in the 1930s. This term suggests that these communities are 'original inhabitants of India'. However, anthropological research has established that at least nine of the ten tribes talked about were formed after the decline of the Indus Valley Civilization around 1800 BCE. The people whose descendants form the present-day tribes came from all parts of the world, and their racial origins can be traced to the Indo-Aryan, Austroasiatic and Tibeto-Burman language groups. The tenth tribe, the Jarawas, remained secluded for more than 25,000 years from the subcontinent. Since there is earlier evidence of both Dravidians and Aryans in the subcontinent, the term 'original inhabitants' would be misleading.

The Constitution of India refers to tribal populations as scheduled tribes. The motivation here was to ensure their development.

In ancient India, tribals were largely outside the caste system. The oldest mention of the tribals is in the epics like Mahabharat and Ramayan. But mostly, the tribal population remained outside the ambit of mainstream life, and the only mentions in various texts are brief ones pertaining to disputes or other interactions. These disputes arose mainly because the tribals were perceived as largely 'uncivilised' and 'different' from the others in terms of appearance, food habits, lifestyle and religion.

The relative autonomy and collective ownership of tribal land by tribal people was first severely disrupted with the advent of the Mughals in the early sixteenth century. While some tribals rebelled, most were pushed deeper into the forests. The historiography of relationships between the tribal people and the rest of Indian society is patchy, with occasional mentions, such as alliances between the Ahom kings of the Brahmaputra valley and the hill Nagas.

Some communities were completely ignored by the administration from the beginning of the East India Company dominance, in 1757, and later by the British government. These communities included the Marias of Bastar due to lack of access and the Konyaks due to geographical disadvantage.

But in other cases, they trampled over tribal systems, as with the Khasis of Meghalaya and Kurumbas of the Nilgiris. This led to rebellions or widespread population decline, as happened with the Jarawas when the British decided to settle in the Andaman islands.

As a result of constant displacement, tribal religions evolved. Each tribe has distinct religious beliefs and practices, sharply distinguished from mainstream religions. They were often animistic in nature, which essentially meant worship of non-human entities like plants, trees and animals. Over the past century, most of these religions have been diluted with practices from Hinduism, Christianity or Islam, or in some cases largely disappeared.

Those who continue to hold on to traditional religions, such as the Kurumbas and Khasis, are protective of them. While rituals like headhunting and animal sacrifice have been given up, some traditions continue, such as the ghotuls of the Marias and sacred groves of the Khasis.

Despite many differences, all the tribes covered in this book, and others, have one thing in common—they are deeply in sync with their environment, understand its rhythm, and know each plant by its uses. They take from nature only what is required and give nature time to heal and re-grow. Whether it is the Kurumbas leaving behind some honey for animals in the jungle or the Khasis preserving tracts of forests for centuries, each tribe treats mother nature with the greatest respect. It is no coincidence that the areas where each of these tribes live are immensely rich in biodiversity, and many plants are conserved in their natural habitats by the magico-religious beliefs of the tribes.

Over the centuries, as each successive invader charged into the subcontinent, the tribes were pushed further back into the shadows, where they learnt to survive on what was available, and were called savages for their unfamiliarity with mainstream life. As populations grow and land becomes scarce, modern encroachments have forced many tribals back into so-called civilised society, which they neither understood nor were prepared for.

In 1958, the then prime minister, Jawaharlal Nehru, formulated the tribal Panchsheel principles to guide government actions. The five principles focused on the non-imposition of alien values, tribal land and forest rights and general respect for tribal life and autonomy.

More recently, the Panchayats Extension to the Scheduled Areas Act of 1996 and the Forest Rights Act of 2006 have given tribals access to restricted areas of the forest to protect their lands and homes. However, this information is not well disseminated to those who are supposed to be the beneficiaries, and many tribals are meted out unfair treatment by government officials, corporate houses and rebels like Naxals.

The fact is, tribals have their own designs for development. For instance, the Konyak villages in Nagaland follow a community-based system, where irrespective of whose field it is, a set of villagers assigned by the village council in Sunday meetings, work together. The Marias have no future tense in the everyday grammar of their language. Their lives function solely on what is relevant today and surrounding them—land, water and forests. And these designs of development is what in a world ravaged by Covid, we all aspire to attain—a cleaner, simpler and greener life.

In India, tribal people have an estimated population of 10.4 crore, which is 8.6 per cent of the population. There are around 645 distinct tribes in India, but there are many more ethnic clusters that would be eligible for the scheduled tribe status, but are not officially recognized. The largest concentrations of Indigenous people are found in the seven northeastern states of India, such as the Khasis, Jaintias, Adis, Mizos, Karbis, Nyishis, Angamis and Konyaks. The next largest is in the so-called central tribal belt that stretches from Rajasthan to West Bengal, namely the Gonds, Bhils, Santhals, and Mundas, among others. While the north has tribes like the Changpas and the Bakarwals, south India has the Chenchu, Kurumbas and Halakkis. Some of the oldest known inhabitants still live in Andamans, with populations so small that they number in double or triple digits, such as the Jarawas, Sentinelese and Andamanese.

The ten tribes in this book represent different cultures from different parts of India, about whom enough primary data is available in terms of anthropological research, interviews or field research. However, in no way should these ten tribes be considered representative of all tribes in general.

Some of the interviews and research were done for my earlier book, *White as Milk and Rice*, which contains records of six of these tribes. These have been adapted and abridged for young readers to enjoy. I hope that you find these essays a rich resource of information about human evolution in India and the lives of one-tenth of people living in the long shadows of our country's centuries-old history.

THE HALAKKIS
of North Karnataka

A tribe where women sing all day long, whether they are walking to the forest or milking their cows—and with changing times, using their tunes to fight for their rights.

A few kilometres from Ankola in Karnataka is Badigeri, a village on the edge of a forest. Just before sunrise—before the men are awake—cooking smoke swirls up from the koppas, or group of huts, and one can hear the chuck-chuck of firewood being chopped. After the women get done with household chores, they head to the forests to gather produce.

A row of barefoot, sari-clad women emerges from the huts. They wear layers of traditional, colourful beads around their neck, all the way down to their shoulder. They help one another to put them on, layering them, and letting the beads intermingle. The beads not only assert their identity, but also help them keep their necks straight as they lift the heavy firewood. Their mouths are stained with betel leaves. On the long walks to the forests, the women begin humming songs. 'Chanda da matgai . . .' they sing, about tying firewood into bundles.

The men work as labourers in the fields and homes of rich men. In their free time, they drink liquor and play the drum. Women, on the other hand, hardly have any free time. They do household chores and gather forest produce in the morning, work in the hot fields in the afternoon, and sell the day's produce in the market by evening. At home, they finish cooking, cleaning, and tending to the cattle before retiring for the day. That is why they sing—to forget the banality of their daily chores and divert their attention away from the aching muscles caused by all the hard work. They have songs for every mood—when they are anxious, excited, content, or sad. A lot of these songs have very similar tunes as these women have no formal training in music.

The Halakki tribals live on the outskirts of towns between the mighty Western Ghats in the east and the expanse of the Arabian Sea in the west, in the Martian red lands of Uttara Kannada (North Karnataka). In spite of living close to other communities, Halakkis remain wary of outsiders as a way of protecting their culture and practices. The men wear only the traditional white loincloth and a turban, and women wear sarees without blouses and layers of beads around their necks. They appear strikingly distinct, so much so that even an outsider can distinguish them from other communities.

On warm spring days, the Halakki's forests look very promising. The wood is dry, with twigs crunching beneath their feet, perfect for tying a decent-sized bundle for firewood. The forests are also laden with berries of different kinds—sweet white ones called murghlannu or mulannu and the tart black ones known as kajalaanu. They are gathered into bundles that women carry on one arm, along with vegetables gathered from the wild. Occasionally, they pick maddale flowers, which are said to cure colds, or brahmi for their husbands, to make their minds sharper. Roots of kakke and kasamarda are stocked for fever.

Medicinal plants and recipes are usually known to one elder in the family, of either gender, who venture alone into the forest in the wee hours of the morning to collect the herbs. A mortar and pestle is used to grind them into fine pastes or powders which are wrapped in leaves for storage. The recipes are imparted only on the deathbed of the elder and passed on orally to sons or daughters-in-law. Many herbal preparations, including those that were allegedly cures for cancer, have disappeared because of this practice.

Halakki folk songs are known as janapadas. They talk about the tribe's bond with nature, the water they drink, and animals they have for playmates. The women spend hours in the forests, spotting a giant mushroom or an iridescent bioluminescent fungus that grows on rotting barks of trees. As they move deeper into the forest, they sing songs about their land's talking trees and gnomes that live in the duffs or decayed matter on the forest floor. There is wildlife aplenty—black panthers perched on high branches, a lone tigress, and herds of elephants—but they watch these women sing and leave them alone. There are almost no records of wild animals attacking the Halakkis. One would like to think that this is because all inhabitants of the forest love the gentle Halakkis, who never take more than what they need from the forest.

On rainy days, the forest isn't very giving. The wood becomes heavy with water and berries are too few, and the women return empty handed. But as dark clouds gather overhead, they put aside all their worries to welcome the rain gods with songs. They forget their roofs are not repaired, that the scant produce from the forest will fetch hardly any money in the market and the moneylenders will soon come knocking on their door. Instead, they sing 'thaarley, thaarley' and perform their traditional rain dance, wishing for rain to come and the land to flourish.

Traditional songs are a big part of Halakki life. They have their own variations of popular mythologies, which have been orally passed from mothers to daughters. For example, Mahabharat is Pandavakami[1] while Ramayana is Seethekami. In these lands, women are the stronger sex, taking care of both work and family unlike their men, and thus Sita is depicted as the hero of their version of the epic. This belief of Halakki women inspires songs for every occasion and relationship.

Sisterhood is one theme these songs focus on, speaking of the tenderness, love and mutual admiration among the women who work together all day. The particularly nasty ones are reserved for a sister-in-law who ruins a relationship between a brother and a sister, leaving a trail of curses for her or wishing upon her an ugly baby. Sexual desire is another subject that is sung of, describing it as they would speak of any other complex emotion.

The Halakkis have oral origin stories, but there is little recorded history. According to Halakki elders, a holati or an outcast woman, once held control over Konkan coastal lands. Lord Shiva wanted a stronger foundation for society. Therefore, he killed the pariah woman and obtained a caste from each of her body parts. When the 'not yet created' Halakkis complained, Shiva created them from the milk and rice he was eating.

---

[1] The Pandavakami refers to the five brothers, Yudhishthira, Bhima, Arjuna, Nakula and Sahadeva, who are the five acknowledged sons of Pandu and central to the epic of Mahabharata.

Another origin story is often sung by women. Parvathi was taking food to the fields where Shiva was working. On the way, she tripped and fell. She gathered the rice and milk pudding into a mound of dolls. Shiva, who was very hungry, touched the dolls to see if they were real and within minutes, they came to life. The dolls thanked him and asked Shiva what they could do for a living. Shiva proclaimed that since they were born while he was ploughing the fields, they should continue as farmers.

Hardly any Halakkis own lands, but every afternoon, all the young Halakki women can be found in fields of jeera (cumin), peanuts, ragi (millet), and other vegetables like water spinach and puni soppu (sorrell). The lower-caste Halakkis (who even today fight for their scheduled caste status with the government) only work in these fields, while the ownership lies with other communities, especially men, known for their quick tempers and large bellies.

The Halakki woman I had interviewed as part of my research, sneakily imitated an upper caste field owner rushing the workers: 'Move your hands faster,' she imitated. 'Look at you, weeding out my crop . . .'

Men and women work together pulling out jungle rice and toothcup weeds, in the searing afternoon heat. The women also do housework in affluent homes or work as porters, doing small chores.

Like many other tribes around the world, the Halakkis used to practise polygamy but nowadays they have largely shifted to monogamy. Weddings among Halakkis are elaborate. Unlike the more commonly prevalent dowry system, where the bride's family pays the groom, the

Halakki groom has to pay a bride price to the bride's father to confirm the wedding. The wedding is agreed upon at a mutually convenient time by placing betel leaves and areca nuts in the palms of the families.

The bride's family is expected to welcome the groom enthusiastically. The men decorate the wedding ceremonial pergola with mango leaves and flowers, while the women make hallis, the traditional form of decorating walls employed during most festivals and rituals. On the wedding day, the bride and groom sit in front of a halli of parrots. Guests are welcomed with satirical songs, making fun of young couples or even in-laws, and they often throw interesting light on their interpersonal relationships.

A popular song that Halakki women sing has a new wife mocking the in-laws—'They didn't even offer jaggery with water; we have wells in our village too.' Offering jaggery with water is a popular tradition among Halakkis. This combination not only quenches thirst but also provides additional nutritional benefits for the hardworking Halakkis. Nowadays, some Halakkis drink tea too, calling it a 'watery milk drink'.

Ragi was traditionally the staple food, but it has now been sidelined by the consumption of soft and fluffy rice, as is more common among upper-caste families. Fish curry is popular, especially when combined with dry pickled fish and vegetables. The food is served on banana leaves with coconut shell spoons.

Births among Halakkis are also full of rituals. As soon as labour pains begin, a *notagara* (priest) comes home and dances with peacock feathers to take the woman's mind off the pain and to ensure a normal delivery. After the village midwives deliver the baby, they pray to the tortoise god, bathe the baby and feed it a pinch of butter and jaggery.

Young Halakki children are put to work to do small tasks like making cow dung cakes for the kitchen stove or helping to feed or wash the cattle. They often accompany their parents to the fields, helping them weed, sow and reap. Traditional children's games include surguddu (kabbadi), balli chippi (a game with a bat and a ball), seashells, stone games and cockfights.

Homes for this hardworking community are only a place to rest after a hard day's work, so they call them 'bidara' or a camp, indicating the temporary nature of the dwellings. Made from straw, stones, mud, fronds and plumes, their homes are surrounded by mango, coconut, banana trees and vegetable beds, especially the Malabar spinach. They carefully nurture many varieties of hibiscus, margosa, and roses, and use them for pujas and decorations. Every home has a tulsi plant which is prayed to before every meal. Halakki songs often fantasize about multi-storeyed homes, an indication of higher status and wealth.

Eh nath tulasi garo
Atalo chomein gardalo
Cheralo atalochomein garodanalo
(Roughly translated: We have brought flowers and mane and doll.
All of it we have brought to you, and chandanna srigandha, sandalwood paste.
Tulsamma, each doll we will decorate, to please you we are doing all this.)

It was earlier assumed by anthropologists that Halakkis migrated from the Andhra region because they are staunch followers of Thirupathi Thimmappa of Tirupati, Andhra Pradesh and their songs often mention the Bay of Bengal. Their language, Achchagannada, also resembles Telugu. Upon their arrival in Karanataka, they stayed around Karwar, choosing to live like the Todas of Nilgiris, near the foothills and forest borders, depending on kumbri[2] agriculture system and often hunting for a living. When the British government debarred slash and burn farming in jungles in the nineteenth century, they gradually migrated out. They lived on riverbanks and seashores, between Honnavar and Karwar, and took up hunting, forest gathering, and agriculture as their main occupations. Daily wage labour was their only major source of income until the government introduced the 'tiller is the owner' scheme in the 1960s and 1970s.[3]

Halakkis, over the last decade, have actively started singing to voice political concerns. They have used songs as a medium of peaceful protest for a patch of land or scheduled caste status or for a government beneficiary

---

[2] In a forest, where land is cleared by burning trees and once the soil's fertility is depleted due to use, they clear another patch of land to grow crops.

[3] Patil, R. V. "'All Land to the Tiller': The Problem of Land Reform in India." *Economic Development and Cultural Change 3*, no. 4 (1955): 374–80. A system of land tenure was introduced, in which actual tillers or cultivators could have ownership or occupancy rights but the paperwork to claim the land was too complicated for the uneducated farmers. In many places where small and marginal farmers leased land from large or absentee landowners, the situation continued to be exploitative, thereby discouraging the actual tillers from cultivating the land efficiently.

scheme. They sing songs of protest on stage, using this powerful ancient tool to bring change. They sing for the education of young girls, banning spurious liquor that has killed many of their men, and for many social changes.

Hunting used to be the way of life for Halakkis until the late twentieth century. It was customary for men to test their skills with hunting. But following various uprisings by villagers during the British rule in 1878, weapons, including those for hunting, were banned. Later with the Forest Rights Act (1927) and the Indian Wildlife Act (1972), hunting was regulated and later completely banned.

Following the various uprisings, the peasants and villagers were denied the possession or use of certain implements and weapons by the British; consequently, they couldn't hunt. With the passing of the Indian Forest Act (1878), forests were classified as 'reserved', 'protected' or 'village'. Hunting was banned in most parts except for certain designated shooting blocks, which were accessible through the acquisition of a licence that was made available to very few people, most of whom were British. To hunt, the requisite permits were to be obtained from the Divisional Forest Officer of the region, who would assign shooting blocks to the applicants, but hunting for food in deeper jungles was still rampant. Due to regulations imposed by the Indian Wildlife Act of 1972, this is now almost non-existent. Earlier, it was necessary for one person from each family to go with the group of villagers to play the hunting game and come back victorious. Hunting was also done around particular festivals, although the practice differs from one region to another.

One Halakki song is about people suffering under the new tax regulation on paddy in the 1970s—about farmers and field workers drinking lake water to remain alive since they are not left with any food to feed their family. The government, in turn, pacifies these women with wads of cash and the men with *ger hand serai,* the local liquor.

Sukiri Bommagowda is a Halakki singer, renowned for her songs and activism. She has worked to preserve traditional songs and to teach these to members of the tribe. She has sung widely on the radio and has espoused many social causes, which she sings about. Famously, she called for ban on alcohol in Uttara Kannada and often speaks up for girls' education, women's rights and financial freedom. She was awarded the Padma Shri in 2017.

Every once in a while, women from NGOs come to the Halakki villages, with the agenda of modernizing and uplifting the tribe, to teach them how to make traditional kokum butter which sells well these days. But the Halakki women only laugh—they know kokum making from their mother's womb, but who would want to sit at home making butter when they can spend their mornings outside in the forest?

Music has the power to change people, Halakki women believe, and endlessly pursue this thought by singing everywhere they go. Throats will be raw, tears will be shed, but above all, they wish to make a powerful and lasting impact, reminding the people where they belong and making sure that they don't forget it themselves.

Current population: 2 lakhs (2011 census)
Languages spoken: Kannada, Achchagannada
Ethnic origin: Some scholars believe them to be the original inhabitants of Uttar Kannada, while others state that the Halakkis migrated from a different region in southern Karnataka.

THE KANJARS
of Chambal Valley

Exploited century after century and once classified as a 'criminal tribe' by law, this north Indian tribe struggles to redefine their identity while looking for newer means of livelihood.

In the ravines of Chambal Valley (southeastern Rajasthan, southwestern Uttar Pradesh, and northern Madhya Pradesh), the edges of rocks are like sharp knives, with the sun glinting off their edges. The shallow and clear Kalsindh River flows alongside. Mayflies appear in hundreds, with eager fish leaping to grab them. Long-billed vultures and hyenas emerge from the sparse forests, pausing at the river for a drink. Little tremors in the waters slowly reveal the sharp snouts of gharials. The Kalsindh River is considered unholy in Hindu traditions. The river is supposedly made from the blood of a hundred cows sacrificed by the mythical Aryan king Rantidev.

The brutal landscape lends its characteristics to the dwellers with whom this area is most often associated—the dacoits of Chambal. Most of them belong to the Kanjar tribe. The name is derived from a general term used for a forest vagabond—the *kan kachar* or one who wanders in the jungle.

The origin story of the Kanjars is that they were once valorous Rajputs fighting for kings and their kingdom's safety. Over centuries, they were pushed into the fringes by multiple invaders. The decisive blow was dealt by Alauddin Khilji (1296–1316), who, after his victory at Chittor in southern Rajasthan in 1303, ruthlessly ordered a massacre of the enemy soldiers. Accounts claim that around 3000 soldiers were cut down. The more fortunate fled into the surrounding forests or hid in the immense ravines further east.

Over time, some of these soldiers settled in surrounding villages and were absorbed into local communities. Others continued to live in the jungles, where robbery became their means of subsistence. They were joined by other outcasts, like people of the untouchable caste, who also felt that the 'Hindu society had rejected them and therefore they rejected the Hindu society'.[4] Some Kanjars therefore have ethnic links, and others who joined because of societal circumstances, and both groups came to be collectively known as Kanjars.

It was not that all Kanjars were dacoits. In 1590, Abu'l Fazl, the Mughal emperor Akbar's court historian, wrote that there were Kanjars in the imperial court. 'Men of this class,' he wrote, 'play the pakhāwaj (drum), the rabāb (lute), and the tāla (cymbals), while the women sing and dance.' Today, many Kanjars own and cultivate the land, but most continue to be involved in various types of socially and formally illicit businesses. It is with professional thievery that the tribe is most associated.

From the earliest mentions in history and folk songs, the Kanjars made the ravines of Chambal their home, having

---

[4] Floris, George A. 'A Note of Dacoits in India', *Comparative Studies in Society and History*, Vol. 4, No. 4 (1962): pp. 467–472

been evicted from Rajput villages by various invaders. Here, the resilient and cunning dacoits eluded the king and, later, both the government and the panchayat. They moved their giroh or a group of closely related families every few months, carrying bundles and boxes and walking briskly from one hideout to another, often covering more than thirty miles in one night.

At a new shelter in the ravines within shrubbery, the Kanjars would rebuild sikris—tents made of sticks and fronds. Wild cats and foxes would idle around them. Their mattresses crawled with bed bugs and the wheat they stole would quickly get infested with weevils. Dried and preserved vegetables along with lentils made a large part of their diet. Women cooked food in pits before dawn to avoid detection from smoke. On days that they anticipated raids, they did not cook.

In these jungle camps, hunger was a common phenomenon. Women brewed *kaccha khatiya*, popularly known as Kanjar whiskey, in the depths of the night. Men finished bottles of this brew to quench their hunger, thirst and frustration. The young boys climbed ber trees and munched on the scarce fruits, holding pretend axes made of bark. From the higher branches, they threw inedible fruits down, making bomb-like sounds with their mouths. Diligently, they chased lizards around the bushes, catching them by their tails and roasting them over the fire. They would run naked around the groves, collecting unusable pieces of loot—boxes, wires, strings, and bags—to trade them. Until an older man caught them by their collars and thrashed them well and dragged them off for training.

When the police passed the camps, young boys were taught to shriek like a peacock as a warning. If a traveller crossed their territory—especially one who looked moneyed—they had to whistle softly, like a white-rumped shama bird. While a few small children were given special training in hiding in holes and under bushes, all were taught to sneak coins and knives in the various orifices of their bodies—mouth, throat, cheeks, and if required, between the cheeks of their bums. Gold, however, could not be hidden below the waistlines.

The older dacoits taught the young boys various techniques of noiselessly digging holes under doors with long iron rods and using the same rod to crack open locks. The Kanjars would rear lizards and use them to determine holes and gaps in doors and walls. Dogs were trained to warn them of strangers and dangers. Befriending street dogs or putting them to sleep with herbs in cold rotis was standard practice.

The Kanjars observe many ritualistic practices. Before every loot, *bhaav* is performed. The men would gather in circles at a secret temple in Rawali, near Kota, Rajasthan. Those who could not go down to the temple, performed the bhaav at home, with the encampment's *bhopa* (priest) presiding. A bhopa would call powerful spirits within himself. A full bottle of liquor would be spun, and the gang would head in the direction in which the bottle pointed when it came to a halt. Larger heists required sacrifices of goats and camels. The Kanjars would dip a thumb in the blood of the carcass and press it to their foreheads. If the spirit in the bhopa predicted poor gains, they cancelled plans and waited for fortunes to turn.

But if the bhaav gave a go-ahead, the women would bring an empty ancestral bowl, often silver or copper, pour in kaccha khatiya, and mix it with sacrificial blood.

The men drank from the bowl, pledging loyalty to the giroh and acceptance of the consequences if there was a breach of trust. The men would close their eyes and kiss the bowl to solemnize the vow. The safety of the gang and the security of the information were always among their top priorities.

Excursions to melas in villages were a cover for reconnaissance, though there could also be stray pilferage of coconuts, shoes, soap and snacks. Women would visit villages on the pretext of selling utensils, sarees and homemade pickles. While the villagers bought the wares, the Kanjars would quickly scan their homes and ascertain the thickness of walls, the location of the master bedroom, assess the jewellery the homeowners wore, and which houses seemed a bit lax on security. The favourite targets were ones where wedding preparations were underway, as there would be precious things aplenty, and people would be too busy to be vigilant.

Later at night, the men would return to the most promising home with some tools. The nights around the new moon were most favoured, as were nights when it was windy, as darkness and the covering noise made their work easier.

On days when there was no looting scheduled, the Kanjars planned their travels, sold the loot through middlemen and worked on their skills.

The elder Kanjars pass on survival tactics to the younger people. If you poison a man with datura seeds after a long hot day, the police will assume it's heat stroke. When using arsenic, remember to burn the cloth you burnt it in. Heal your burns after injuries by dipping in cold cow dung. Use herbs like gudbel (tinospora cordifolia), kali musli (curculigo orchioides gaertn), dholi musli (white musli), ashwagandha (withania somnifera), shilajit (a blackish-brown powder from mountain rocks), and turmeric. Don't rob when you can steal. If necessary, kill.

Chaurasi Buddhiyan, or the eighty-four wisdoms, is an oral text of unknown antiquity, which serves as the essential handbook for Kanjars. It is full of rules, modi operandi, ancestral practices and regulations of matters. There were other rules to ensure a successful dacoity—abstaining from sexual intercourse before a loot, taking a bath and praying to the Din Devata.

The code of conduct was of utmost importance. They were, after all, Rajputs by descent, and the cardinal virtue that Rajputs claim to embrace is heroism. The greatest fear for Kanjars was not death, but divulgence of the gupt pachan, or the secrets of their community. This festering fear underlies their every thought and activity.

Sultana Daku was a famous Bhatu dacoit (Bhatus are a subtribe of Kanjars) at the turn of the twentieth century. He roamed the jungles and ravines of the then United Provinces—looting, plundering, and murdering with impunity. He had a terrifying career but was regarded as Robin Hood by his tribesmen because he shared his loot and took care of their grievances. Finally, captured by a British police officer Freddie Young (reputed to be the fattest officer in India) in Nainital, he was hanged in 1924. Young was feted by the British as the hero of the Rohilkhand region.[5]

---

[5] Saraf, Sujit. *The Confession of Sultana Daku*. New Delhi: Penguin Books, 2009

Popular British interest in thugee had been sparked by *Confessions of a Thug* (1839), a novel by Philip Meadows Taylor, and three non-fiction tomes on the subject by William Henry Sleeman, later the Commissioner for the Suppression of Thugee and Dacoity. *Confessions of a Thug* caught Queen Victoria's fancy and was read as fact, though undoubtedly fiction. The horror of thugees was codified into law by the Thugee Acts of 1836–48.

Sleeman also wrote of the newly discovered 'fraternities of hereditary robbers' and vowed to 'finish the menace'. It is believed he said that, 'If you have a very sweet dog that bites children, you have to choose the children, and put the dog down.'

The British government, therefore, enacted the Criminal Tribes Act (1871, 1911, 1924) which criminalized entire communities by designating them as habitual criminals. Under these acts, ethnic or social communities in India, were defined as 'addicted to the systematic commission of non-bailable offences', such as theft. Adult males in the groups were forced to report weekly to the local police station and had restrictions imposed on their movements. They were among those designated criminal tribes. The Kanjars were described as 'a tribe whose ancestors were criminals, who are themselves destined by usages of caste (system of India) to commit crimes and whose descendants will be offenders against the law until the whole tribe is exterminated or accounted for in the manner of thugs.' The law said, 'If the local government has the reason to believe that any tribe, gang, or class of person is addicted to the systematic commission of non-bailable offences, it may report to the Governor-General in council, and may request his permission to declare such tribe, gang or class a criminal one.'[6]

As a result of these Acts and the administrative horror of 'hereditary robbers', Kanjar camps were raided and all members of the giroh were thrown into criminal colonies, where they were closely monitored by the police. The Salvation Army, an international charitable organization with affiliations to the church, tried to convert Kanjars or hired them in cottage industries where they were given moral lectures and alternative low-paying jobs. Many families ran away and driven by necessity, became involved in more organized crime.

After Independence, the Indian parliament replaced the Criminal Tribes Act with the Habitual Offenders Act (1952). But far from improving their lives, the new Act only made others treat them poorly and unfairly. They were exploited by the police—robberies and loots in neighbourhoods would be immediately attributed to those Kanjars living close to them. This pushed them to rebel, turn more fearsome and often find solace in the brotherhood of the tribe.

Vinoba Bhave (1895–1982), an advocate of non-violence and human rights, tried an innovative approach to this problem. In 1960, Bhave ventured into the Chambal to persuade the dreaded dacoits to give up violence. At a public meeting, he said, 'I have come to the glorious land of the brave. This is the land that has produced brave dacoits. They are noble men. The only difference between them and other men is that their train has got on to the

---

[6] Act XXVII of 1871, also known as the Criminal Tribes Act [later repealed].

wrong track.'[7] He urged them to try an alternate life, with complete security from the government. Around twenty dacoits are said to have surrendered to Vinoba.

Today, several 'ex-criminal' and ex-nomadic tribes, such as the Pardhis, Bhats, Bhantus, Barbarias, Kanjars and Vanjaris, continue to be seen as a threat to settled villages. They may have moved out of the jungles, but they still live in separate encampments outside the villages, hidden behind long cobs of corn fields, tall trees, or ravines.

Flies perch atop their kurtas as they make kaccha khatiya in the dark shadows of moonless nights. The illegal brew fetches them a living besides their meagre savings from the sale of the cash crops. So deep is their fear of the police that their belongings are never on the shelf— scissors, pens, clothes and ID cards are always together in bundles or boxes. They may not be nomads anymore, but habits are hard to break.

Social rejection is continuous. Upper-caste Hindus sprinkle purifying water when they pass by. When Kanjar encampments are considered too close to a village, the villagers often destroy or burn the encampment. Even the poorest villagers refuse to take work from them. 'They are subjected to headcounts on account of their being considered habitual offenders by the state,'[8] or their settlements are made close to the police station. Even today, these so-called criminal tribes

---

[7] Rajgopal, P.V. *The British, the Bandits and the Bordermen: From the Diaries and Articles of K.F. Rustamji*. New Delhi: Wisdom Tree, 2020.
[8] Sharma, Sudhirendar. 'India Must Scrap the Law That Tags Some Tribes as Hereditary Criminals'. *Hindustan Times,* 1 November 2017.

become easy substitutes for criminals whom the police fail to detain.

Forced to remain in the fringes, the Kanjars look for alternative means of livelihood when denied jobs and land for irrigation. Do we continue to stigmatize them wrongly? This is a question we need to answer urgently. Because not answering this question means that we continue to let our fellow citizens be victims of injustice even seven decades after independence.

Current population: 115,968 (2011 census)
Languages spoken: Narsi, Marwari, Punjabi
Ethnic origin: Rajputs (Indo-Aryans)

THE KONYAK NAGAS
of Nagaland

A tribe of traditional head-hunters living in mist-covered mountains and preserving ways of life reminiscent of more adventurous times.

As one swerves around mountains in Nagaland, the wind rakes over green rice fields and in some secluded stretches, the lollipop colours of the opium-rich poppies. To reach Mon, in the north of Nagaland, one has to drive for hours on narrow dust and stone-mule paths winding across the lofty ranges that weave their way to Burma. On either side, hundreds of kilometres of thick jungles of bamboo and palms creep up the steep slopes of the Patkai Hills, which divide the region from the rest of India.

The word 'Naga' as a collective name for the various tribes who live in the Naga Hills dates back to British times. The thirty-six tribal groups of these hills knew themselves by their distinct tribe names, not as a collective. But these particular Nagas in Mon district came to be known as Konyaks, traditionally known as the fiercest of the Naga tribes, easily recognizable from their facial tattoos.

There are many theories about the origins of the Konyak Nagas. Their headhunting traditions are similar to those of the Dayaks[9] of Malaysia. Their language is Sino-Tibetan, the second-largest language group in the world by origin. There is no written historical record extant about their origin and the route of migration to their present habitation. Hiuen Tsang, the Chinese pilgrim who visited Assam in 645 CE during the reign of Bhaskar Varman (600-650 CE), mentioned that the inhabitants of the border hills showed similarities to the barbarians of southwest China. Some scholars claim that the existence of the Nagas is mentioned by Claudius Ptolemy, the Greek scholar, in his *Geographia* (c. 150 CE) as the land of the naked people, and the location he alludes to is that of present-day Nagaland.

Some scholars believe that the Nagas immigrated from three directions—north-east Asia, north-west Asia and south-east Asia. Oral traditions passed from generation to generation narrate that the ancestors of the Konyaks came from a mythical peak called Yengyudang. Another folktale tells of migration from mainland China via the Brahmaputra valley along the Dikhu river into the hills

---

[9] The Dayaks are the native people of Borneo. It is a loose term for over 200 riverine and hill-dwelling ethnic subgroups, located principally in the central and southern interior of Borneo. The Dayaks were animist in belief; however, many converted to Islam. Since the nineteenth century, the Dayaks were feared for their ancient tradition of headhunting practices. The Iban Dayaks (a sub-group of the Dayaks) believe that the origin of headhunting was a mourning ritual, as instructed by a spirit. The secured head would retain the characteristics of the person whose head was taken and protect them from territorial conquests.

flanking it. The prosaic consensus is that the Nagas immigrated from South Asia through the corridor of the Indo-Myanmar border to the Naga Hills.

As one drives along the tracks, every once in a while, one passes a lone Naga person walking down the hills with a basket on their backs with machetes and produce from the field or forest. Despite the long stretches of jungle, animals are rarely visible. One lone mithun (Drung ox) is visible almost a two-hour drive to the village near Longwa—the last wild east frontier of India. Seeing the car, it gallops back into the forest. Elephants are almost extinct here. Monkeys that casually hang on the rails by the road in hills elsewhere in India prefer the treetops in these dense thickets. They seem to fear the Konyaks, a Naga tribe whose homes lie here and there, in the shadows of the forest, lost in time.

In this tiny Konyak village near the Indo-Burma border, enormous trees stretch their gnarled branches against the sky. The impenetrable undergrowth makes it tough to walk. On the top of hills, open to all storms, bamboo houses cling to the rocks.

At the entrance to the village is the morung. This is the boys' dormitory, where boys and young men are trained for wars and prepared for village festivals, hunting expeditions and other social engagements. In most villages, the morung now lies empty, except for a massive fifteen-feet log drum made from a hollow log of wood used to make announcements.

Up in the hills, the Konyaks lead a busy life. The grandparents and older siblings take care of the babies and the home, while the rest of the adults go to the fields.

Often, villagers in Mon hold both Indian and Burmese citizenship—while many children in Longwa go to school in Burma, a few living on the Burmese side of the border work for the Indian army.

The Konyaks here have a community-based approach to farming. The village council meets every Sunday to decide which group of people works in which field, irrespective of the ownership of the fields. The group moves from field to field—weeding, planting and harvesting. They practise jhum agriculture, where a piece of land or forest land is cleared, burnt, and then used for cultivation. The workers have time for only two meals a day and a few rounds of opium.

In the villages, outside each house, there is usually a bamboo shanty with pigs and roosters. A village elder sits outside his home—he has black teeth, and cheeks lined with tattoo ink. Until the first half of the twentieth century, Konyaks believed that only animals had white teeth.

The bamboo huts are usually two-roomed and windowless, with the door as the single source of light. In most houses, there is a rack above the central kitchen fire, from which pork, chicken, taro and tapioca hang to be smoked and stored for the winter. A ruddy fire is constantly lit in both rooms to keep the caterpillars and moss away and the room warm. On the bamboo walls, machetes, daos or axes, and guns shine in the darkness.

In many houses, a small figurine of Jesus stands on a shelf, along with a packed copy of the Bible. The advent of Christianity to these hills from the nineteenth century onwards has changed many things. Over the last few decades, more Konyak families have given in to the pressure of going to the church in the nearby village, if not completely converting to Christianity. Until the early 1900s, the Konyaks were animists, which meant, among other things, that they believed that there was consciousness in natural phenomena and in some inanimate objects.

On the exterior walls of the huts hang skinned heads of bulls, bears, deers, and rats. The heads are boiled before being hung. The Konyaks believe that hanging heads outside their homes brings prosperity to the village and makes men stronger, giving them divine powers to fight enemies.[10] Earlier, similarly treated human heads would hang in their place. Now, the human heads lie covered in a ditch down the hills. While headhunting was banned in 1962, among the Konyaks it allegedly persisted for some more years. The last reported case was in August 1990, following a land dispute between the Konyak and Chang tribes.

The Konyaks are martial and territorial and each village fought for its land. The elders would tell the young ones to eat with a spear in their hand as the enemy wouldn't wait for them to finish eating before attacking. The traditional

---

[10] The Nagas of Nagaland and their land and resources are protected under Article 371A of the Indian Constitution, which is a special provision with respect to the state of Nagaland. Special powers and autonomy are given to the Konyak tribe in this region to conduct their own affairs through the village council, a panchayat of sorts. Article 371A states that: (1) Notwithstanding anything in this Constitution, (a) no Act of Parliament in respect of (i) religious or social practices of the Nagas, (ii) Naga customary law and procedure, (iii) administration of civil and criminal justice involving decisions according to Naga customary law, (iv) ownership and transfer of land and its resources, shall apply to the State of Nagaland unless the Legislative Assembly of Nagaland, by a resolution, so decides.

belief was that to survive, a village must grow bigger and stronger. For that, enemies' heads must be brought to the village and fed rice beer. This would bring the village wealth and the head-hunter, recognition, and virility. The greater the number of heads hunted, the greater the respect for the hunter. Each head hunted was marked by a ceremonial tattoo on the head hunter's face.

Their constant desire for territory and resources often put the Konyaks in conflict with their immediate neighbours. They produced sophisticated weapons, like bombs and guns, in their homes. Their neighbours in Assam and Burma, and later the British, were wary of their fierce guerrilla warfare, which included an intimidating invocation of wild animals, the sun, moon and earth and other magical elements, a tribute to their animistic beliefs. In the Konyak value system, the death of a relative or even of anyone from the same village had to be avenged, which caused constant wars between villages.

Till the eighteenth century, wars were fought with expertly made spears, bows and arrows, and dao swords, which, with a single movement, could cut down the head of the enemy. But the desire for better weapons led to the invention of muzzle-loading guns. Nagas claim they were the first ones in the world to make guns, though the oldest gun in the world is dated back to the twelfth century, invented by the Chinese. It was a rudimentary weapon, with a barrel and trigger made of iron extracted from the riverside. Ten or twelve could be manufactured with iron collected in a year. Wars turned more savage and bitter.

Bullets were made from coins, and gunpowder was prepared from a combination of tree bark mixed with ammonia from crystallized human urine.

Unlike the rest of India, where guns are illegal, almost every Konyak has a rudimentary gun, even today.[11] In wide-open patches among the hillock homes, plum-cheeked, sunburnt boys play with pretend bamboo guns. The boys rush towards the opposing team, often from the neighbouring village. A boy from the losing team sits on his knees, while the tallest boy from the winning team pretends to knock him down and then breaks into a dance, hopping like a bird from one foot to another.

There is a strong sense of community in the village. Meetings are held among the villagers about the allocation of community duties. All villagers are obliged to help one another in wars, in the fields, for building or rebuilding houses, and during festivals, weddings and other social occasions.

Upto the first half of the twentieth century, when morungs were used as training spaces, the older men would sit about the hut, sharpening their spears or mending hunting nets, while the younger men manned the village outposts and bunkers. The morungs had no formal heads, but the valorous and the experienced took the lead. The older men would counsel the younger warriors constantly, even, for example, when they would be on a two or three day trek to an enemy village—'If you fight when that feeling of anger is on top of your mind, you'll expose yourself, and it will be easy for the enemy to kill you.'

---

[11] Getting gun licences in Nagaland used to be a lot easier than in the rest of India. One can also procure a permit to buy a greater number of bullets than is allowed in the other states of India.

The Anghs are traditional chiefs or kings of each fiefdom, or a bunch of villages. They were held in high esteem, more as traditional figures of authority rather than decision makers.

The boys of the morung worked together in the fields, went on hunting expeditions and practised war skills. The older boys taught the younger ones to build bunkers, extract poison from certain trees in the forest to make arrows, and most important of all, to hate their enemies intensely—to prepare themselves for a life of fighting as a naomei or warrior.

There was a formal initiation ceremony when a boy became a naomei. It involved, among other things, sacrificing a pig and singing a traditional song:

'Hhi, hi, hi, ha, ha, ha, yu my shi mei enek mu shi mei kheang phe' (rough translation: 'May my rice beer increase, may my rice become plentiful; may all enemies, all head-takers, and all kings eat from my rice.') Copious amounts of rice beer would be drunk. There would also be ceremonial dancing around posts, elaborately carved with elephants, hornbills, tigers, and a peculiarly elongated, erect penis.

The war strategy of the Konyaks had a certain pattern. Groups would travel to the enemy village, carrying the morung drum. They moved in single file, up and down the valleys, with stones rolling at their heels and grey clouds crowding in. Steep slopes and heavy rainfall meant swollen streams. The almost perpetual mist in these hills camouflaged movements, though sometimes this also hid enemy villages. At night, they slept under large rocks with spears by their side. They would carry rice wrapped in banana leaves packed by their wives or mothers. These had to be cooked inside holes covered with charcoal embers to avoid smoke that could warn the enemies. Sometimes they'd just eat preserved smoked meat or sniff out spots that produced well-developed taro roots. They ate what they could hunt along the way—monkey heads, cat tails and yak belly.

A group of ten to twelve strong young men would attack first. If they sounded a call for help, others waiting in the dugouts outside would join them. As the battle started, both sides would sing war songs to heighten their resolve—'We killed your brother, and he was a coward' goes one such song. As the first blood was shed, there would be a great shout of victory. The victim's hair would be pulled tight, and the head sliced off. Men would be hung from trees. Once the heads were cut off, the bodies would be hurled into the gloomy ravines. Fighting would continue until one of the morung gangs sounded the gong—a low, deep, echoing sound of mourning. Ivory was offered as a sign of surrender. The vanquished would have their weapons confiscated, including helmets made of bear skin, bows and arrows, and guns.

The British in India first encountered the Nagas in 1832, when Captains Jenkins and Pemberton, along with 700 soldiers and 800 coolies, marched across the Naga Hills to find a route from Manipur to Assam. They occupied Papoolongmai in the face of fierce resistance by the Angami Nagas.

Over the next fifty years, there were periodic skirmishes and battles between the Nagas and the British. In 1850, the Naga fort of Khonoma fell into the hands of British troops. The British policy of non-interference between 1851 and 1866 emboldened Naga raids into the Assam Valley.

Every morung was a nation unto itself. The war-hungry Nagas raided the British troops from different villages; cheap heads of defenceless warriors were only too welcome. In case of retaliation from the British, they posted sentinels around villages to protect their homes, fields, and sheep pens. The forests were lined with spiked bamboo traps called panjers that could pierce the feet and there were strings that released poisoned arrows straight into the victim's ribs. It is said that a certain British officer once lost three of his troops when they fell into a concealed pit full of large spears.

The British gained control over many Naga territories, but the Konyaks were never defeated. After multiple ambushes in the 1800s, the British gave up, stationing themselves lower in the hills and planting opium close to the Konyaks, hoping, in vain, to numb their savagery. They were successful to a certain extent, as many anghs or kings, gained access to an overwhelming amount of opium, which slowly gained popularity among the commoners too, along with rice beer. But Nagaland was still independent when the British left India, and the state of Nagaland came into existence only in 1963.

A majority of these wars started ostensibly for skulls. Anthropologists have debated whether the later wars happened for deeper, underlying causes, such as land procurement or food. Politically, headhunting is believed to have its significance because in such raids, the defeated villages became the subjects of the victorious village and therefore they had to pay tributes also known as 'poon'. But the warriors themselves, when asked to name a cause of war, usually pointed to the skull. The highlanders, for whom cultivation is a lot of hard work in the mountains, are chronically starved for food, which the skull would ensure aplenty.

The killing was like a graduation ceremony, with the trophies of bloody heads in their basket, and revenge won, the warriors made the first trip to the angh's home. The cleaned heads were laid before him and then skinned. They drank a great deal of rice alcohol to celebrate the victory as tales of the war were recounted to the villagers and dancing went on far into the night. Womenfolk would prepare the festive feast, with beads covering their naked breasts and an apron covering their middle. Log drums would be beaten for hours in the morung. Sometimes the women took turns if the men were too drunk on rice beers. A shaman would be called to speak to the spirits.

The angh's wife, or the queen, would administer the tattoos for the victorious warriors, which could take up to two weeks. The women would go to the jungles to find the red cedar tree, make a dent in its trunk and collect the oozing sap. The sap would be charred and thickened into blueish tattoo ink. The queen would do the tattooing in her home. She would lightly prick the skin with a tool made from thorn bushes, while the skin was stretched by an assistant. The dents were then coated with the tattooink for the blue-black pigmentation that had a healing effect on the punctures too. Almost every victorious warrior got a tattoo, and those who assisted with the killing or performed heroic deeds got a few extra lines on their face.

According to an account a Konyak warrior shared with me during our interviews in 2018, long after the shaman left, they discovered the spirit had not gone back—it screeched, echoed along the valley, blew up their roof and threw a cat over the hill. The angh of the Sheanghag Chingnyu bandaged his head in a fox hide to soften the sound and fastened the shrivelled paws beneath his jawbone. With most warriors still not home, he was afraid for his life. 'It was gone by the time we approached the climb to the village,' the warrior recounted. 'The windy ghost must have seen them arrive with skulls, dripping with blood.'

Today, violence is forbidden among the Konyak Nagas. The church condemns any talk of war and the past. The new religion is considered a rebirth, and nothing of the old ways should remain with a person who is born again.[12]

Over the turn of the twenty-first century, the Nagas may have shed animist ceremonies for Christian ritual, replaced colourful weaves for t-shirts and shorts, and rejected folksongs for carols. But the nights still hold a particular terror for the Konyaks, even after so many decades since the end of headhunting. Children and women are rushed in as soon as darkness descends. Even the bravest warriors sit by the kitchen hearth.

---

[12] Konyak, Phejin. *Last of the Tattooed Headhunters*. New Delhi: Roli Books, 2017.

The homes are still dark, with corners to hide in and a constant fire.

Current population in India: 284,000 (2011 Census)
Ethnic origin: Immigrated from South Asia through the corridor of the Indo-Myanmar border.
Language: Konyak language

THE CHANGPAS
of Changthang

A peaceful Buddhist tribe of herders in one of the highest places in the world.

At altitudes of 13,000 to 190,000 feet, where winter temperatures can drop to minus forty degrees, is a vast desert sandwiched between the Himalayas and the Karakoram range. The Changthang Plateau (alternatively spelled Changthang or Qangtang) is one of the most uninhabitable places on the planet. It is a part of the high altitude Tibetan Plateau in western and northern Tibet extending into the southern edges of Xinjiang, China as well as south-eastern Ladakh, with vast highlands and giant lakes. From eastern Ladakh, the Changtang stretches approximately 1,600 kilometres east into Tibet, as far as modern Qinghai.

On a day when the sky glitters like the turquoise-studded hats of the assembled guests against a theatrical backdrop of lofty mountains, Waze Tshering is married to two brothers,[13] as is the Changpa tradition. On the last day of the three-day wedding gathering, men go horse racing,

[13] Dolkar, Tashi and Azim, Hummara. 'Culture and Cultural Relevance of Changpa Nomads'. *IMPACT: International Journal of Research in Humanities, Arts and Literature*, 2017.

and later they dance with women. The Changpas look stunning in their robes and Chinese masks, as the dust from the horses' hooves flies over the high plains. The celebrations continue late into the night with arrack, the local liquor, and goat meat by the moonlit salt-water lake, near which they have pitched their woollen tents. The following day, the married threesome is left alone while the rest of the tribe returns to their everyday routines.

Nights on this barren plateau are very quiet and still. It is said that every whisper, every laugh, and every Changpa heartbeat can be heard.

The Changpas are pastoral nomadis. It is estimated that there are over half a million nomads living in Changtang. Unlike many other nomadic tribes, the Changpa are not under pressure from settled farmers, as most of the land they inhabit is not suitable for farming.

The Changpas of Ladakh consist of four tribes known as the Kharnakpas, the Rupshupas, the Korzokpas, and the Anghoams, who are further divided into fourteen groups, with an average of one hundred odd families per group. The four usually travel in their own defined territories. Even within each tribe, each family group usually chooses a different grassland so that one herd does not mix with the others.

The camps of the Changpas consist mainly of rebos, tents for human habitation, and corral, goat pens. The rebos are like toy houses, close to one another, but not close enough to be intrusive. Inside the tents, men and women have separate areas. While women may enter the men's areas, the reverse does not happen.

The morning starts with a tribeswoman carrying incense to offer its holy smoke to the livestock in the corrals. The men release the herd from the corrals. The calves are taken away from their mothers, whom the women milk. After this, the herders take the flocks, accompanied by guard dogs, out to the mountain to graze. The herders communicate with their flocks with *whee-whee* and *hurr-hurr* sounds, and the livestock responds by changing directions as asked.

Meanwhile, back at the camp, smoke swirls around the brightly coloured flags decorating the roofs of the rebos. As the morning meal of tsampa (a glutinous meal made from roasted flour, usually barley flour and sometimes wheat flour, eaten with salty Tibetan butter tea) cooks on the stove, tribe members gather around to sit on their haunches, sipping on gur-gur chai, the salty buttery tea. The women shake goatskin bags on their laps to churn the rich fermented yak's milk into slightly cheesy butter. The children, with names like No-No and Po-Po, are called away from playing with new-born foals to eat tsampa mixed with butter.

Women spend a lot of their day outside—washing clothes by the stream or making goat yoghurt or bread, aided by their kids. Younger women and children collect dried dung for fuel. Older men mend bridles or spin the prayer wheels. The family unit is nuclear, and older people, who cannot travel independently, live in villages close to the gompas or Buddhist monasteries, in the region.

Changpas see themselves as Tibetan Buddhists and blend practices of various forms of Buddhism into something uniquely their own. They believe gods reside within humans, and if one strays from one's tribe, one angers the gods. Photos of the Dalai Lama adorn each tent, with butter lamps before them. They pray and light the lamp every day.

Each family owns hundreds of goats and sheep. The best of sheep, horses, goats, and yaks—which are strong, healthy, and of pure breed—are dedicated to the gods and cannot be killed, sold or sheared. The gentle Changpas thus preserve rare precious breeds and prevent their extinction.

While the herd grazes, the men light a fire, sing songs, make butter tea, or munch on Tibetan snacks. They always carry a yurdo, a slingshot, by their side, to scare away any predator, without hurting them. If you see a Changpa shepherd in the mountains, his short and energetic trot matches that of the animals he is herding. The animals are covered in shining fur and the shepherd is clad in moccasins and shawls made from the same fur.

The Changpas depend on their flocks to find grazing spots, eat their meat, and drink their milk. They and their herds of sheep, goats and horses are interdependent and walk and live together each day. The rhythms of Changpa life are planned around the animals and their feeding and rearing schedules. Even when there is a blizzard or cold rain, or when temperatures dip to their lowest, the shepherds continue to take their livestock for grazing.

The tribe divides itself into two groups—Yulpa, or village dwellers, and Changpa, or desert dwellers. The racial group that the Changpas belong to is Tibetan, so they are not that different from other Ladakhis in customs and religion. The language spoken by the Changpas is Changskat.

With no access to satellite weather forecasts, the Changpas rely on their finely attuned senses, honed through centuries of experience. They can tell from gentle changes in the direction of the wind, a slight yellowing of the grass or lengthening shadows on a cliff that it is time to move to greener valleys and pastures. With February temperatures dropping to as low as minus thirty-eight degrees Celsius in the mountains, reading the weather accurately can become a matter of life or death.

When the tribe begins its annual migration to lower lands before winter sets in, the caravan starts at dawn. The livestock leads the way, closely followed by women with babies tied to their backs and children. Men range along the length of the caravan, some on horseback. Except for a few charred marks on the ground where the stoves and fireplaces had been, there is nothing left at the campsite, where the tribe had stayed for many months since spring.

As the caravan weaves its way around the windswept plateau, national borders are often disregarded if they lie on ancient routes. Changpas sometimes wander into Tibetan villages, and the border authorities turn a blind eye. The Changpas might stay for some days, buying glass, plates, velvet and turquoise in exchange for pashmina and cheese.

To Changpas, the pashmina goats are their wealth. In spring months, after the snow melts, they go back up in the hills, where the goats are taken down for shearing, as the hair is no longer needed to keep the body warm. The fleece is sheared in parts over several days so that the goats can slowly adjust to temperature changes. The sheared wool is beaten with sticks to make the fur fluffy and plump. Dust and pests are removed, and the wool is thoroughly sunned. A small celebration with meat and drinks is held after offerings are made at the monastery.

The next stage is the spinning of the wool using a spindle. Weaving holds huge importance in Changpa life and determines a woman's status. Women with good weaving skills not only win much respect from their peers and earn well but also attract many suitors. A hardworking and dedicated woman is most cherished by Changpas.

Women make their own clothing, always dyed in the shade of maroon. They wear a long robe called a goncha, tied by a sash around the waist. A blanket, yogar, covers the shoulders, which not only adds warmth, but helps in carrying babies or other heavy loads.

While both women and men weave goat and sheep fur, traditionally, only men weave yak hair. After shearing, washing, beating, and spinning, a heddle loom is used to weave the brown hair, which varies in colour from charcoal and sepia to deep umber. The woven hair is stitched and assembled into rebos and other utility fabrics. Men also make saddles for horses, blankets, and bags with both goat and yak fibre.

Every Changpa man develops his own distinctive pattern of light and dark lines while weaving, which is like a signature design. This specific design is then passed on to the eldest child, and later the eldest grandchild. Whoever inherits a design makes minute changes to it, to stamp it as his own.

Most of what the Changpas need is provided by nature. The main source of food is derived from livestock. Clothes, tents, and blankets are made from hides and furs. When other produce such as barley, sugar, and rice is required for tsampa, that is when the Changpas need to interact with the outside world. They bring their finest, most desired pashminas and hides, and barter them for utensils and food. The Changpas sell livestock only to control the herd size, when their herds grow too big to sustain.

The wool from a pashmina goat is between fourteen-seventeen microns, unlike the finest sheep's wool which is about twenty-three microns. (Human hair is fifty microns, thrice as thick as pashmina hair.) The less the micron value, the softer and warmer the fabric made from it. Pashmina shawls and sweaters are soft, very warm and light, and sold at higher prices compared to other kinds of woollen garments.

Pashm, the soft fluffy hair secured from the underbellies of pashmina goats, was the most desired product in the heyday of trade along the Silk Route (second century BCE to fourteenth century CE). It was the most exported item from India, through Tibet and then all the way to Turkey and Europe. Zorawar Singh Kahluria (1784–1841) attacked Ladakh in 1834, to gain access to this wool for Raja Gulab Chand of Jammu, and his overlord Emperor Ranjit Singh. When Zorawar tried to conquer Tibet, the bitter cold, hail, snow, and thunderstorms made his soldiers succumb to frostbite. The Tibetans then received help from the Chinese to overcome the threat.[14]

China continues to intervene in the region, now to not only claim land but also to attack the pashmina trade.

[14] Wayman, Frank Whelon and Sarkees, Meredith Reid. *Resort to War: 1816–2007*. Michigan: Sage Publications, 2010.

Pashmina is an expensive wool, so people who cannot afford it buy synthetic pashmina, made in China. The markets in Ladakh are flooded with fake pashmina making it tougher for Changpas to sell their wool.[15]

When the announcement for demonetisation was made in 2016, the Changpas were among the last communities to know. Many couldn't change their notes due to lack of access to banks, while many lost out on trade to rush back into the valleys for financial help. Their nomadic life seems harder than ever to keep up with, and increasingly, young ones choose stable jobs over their ancestral lifestyle.

Changpa children are often lured by the non-nomadic life with televisions and phones. They crave the kind of education that their contemporaries in cities have. The camps are often bereft of teens, who, over the years, have settled in Leh, choosing comfort over the life of a nomad.

The rest of the clan, however, continues to traverse the tough terrains through days of drought and thick snow, through wars and bombing, through modernisation and changing times with their goats in tow, doing what they have been doing for generation after generation—preserving tradition.

Current population: Around 5000 people
Languages spoken: Changskhat
Origin: Tibet and China

---

[15] Guo, Rongxing. *China's Regional Development and Tibet*. Beijing: Springer, 2016.

THE ALU KURUMBAS
of Tamil Nadu, Karnataka and Kerala

Allegedly, descendants of the Pallava kings, the Kurumbas are a tribe of magical honey hunters, who live in the idyllic Nilgiris. But rivalry with other more progressive tribes has curbed the happy lifestyle.

The rolling blue hills of the Nilgiris near the Kerala-Tamil Nadu border, with a gentle breeze bending the tea bushes, are breathtakingly gorgeous. Thrushes chase each other, cicadas orchestrate music in the forest, and monkeys noisily munch a feast on fruit-laden trees.

As dusk sets in, the small hidden hamlet near Coonoor comes aglow with kerosene lamps and kitchen fires. This Kurumba hamlet has sixteen homes. There is no electricity, though it has been available in the next village of Badaga tribals, for years. In the Kurumba hamlet, only a few women wear blouses with their sarees. Men wear more conventional shirts and trousers, in another attempt to look like the more affluent Badagas. The Kurumbas speak a tribal language of their own, which incorporates elements of Tamil, Malayalam and Kannadiga.

The hills of the Nilgiris have historically hosted many tribes—Todas, Badagas, Kotas and Kurumbas. This chapter focuses on the Alu Kurumbas.

The Kurumbas claim to be descendants of the Pallava dynasty, once powerful throughout southern India. When the Pallavas were finally defeated by the Chola ruler Aditya I (c. 870/71 – c. 907 CE), the Kurumbas scattered far and wide. Many fled to the hills in and around the Nilgiris. Scattered among the other Dravidian clans with whom they dwell, the Kurumbas are regarded as some of the oldest inhabitants of the Indian subcontinent, and perhaps, 'contest with their Dravidian kinsmen, in the priority of occupation of the Indian soil.'[16]

Over the centuries, plainsmen like the Badagas poured into the hills, competing for land and resources with native tribes like the Kurumbas. An agriculturist tribe, the Badagas flourished from the 1850s when the British started turning large tracts of natural forests into coffee, tea, pine and eucalyptus plantations. During this period, the Kurumbas continued dwelling in the jungles.

When they appeared around Badaga settlements, word would spread through their village, and Badaga women and children would run for the safety of their homes. The Badagas believed that the Kurumbas had medicines that could put the entire Badaga village to sleep. That Kurumba sorcerers, odikara, could make openings in the fence and the Badaga livestock, under his spell, would follow him through it. That odikaras could turn into bears and

---

[16] Oppert, Gustav Salomon. *On the Original Inhabitants of Bharatavarsa or India*. Andesite Press, 2015.

kill people, just as they knew how to counter spells and prevent misfortune.

Folklore says that once upon a time, a Badaga elder returned breathless from the Kurumba settlement situated outside the jungles, where he had gone to scout a plot for planting tea. He was stuttering incoherently about a big brown monstrous animal, which was no true animal but a Kurumba turned into a monster, and that the end was near. That night, the cows, goats and hens were restless and howled in their sheds, confirming to the villagers that there was indeed a strange presence around. The villagers, too, slept fitfully, imagining lurking shapes in the hilly darkness. The Badagas all knew that it was a Kurumba sorcerer casting spells, and they wondered if he could be appeased with rice, oil, salt and clothes.

Even today, the Badaga elders fear the sorcerer Kurumbas, often banding against them. Their school-going children, meanwhile, have lesser faith in their magical abilities.

> The odikara is a sorcerer. The kanigararu is said to heal diseases with the help of community gods. The devagararu helps other tribes heal with the help of spirits and ancestors. The odigararu uses 'mysterious' air to ward off diseases. The many kinds of magicians suggest how important a role magic plays in tribal culture.

For the last two centuries, especially after 1947, the government imposed restrictions to protect native forests and wildlife. This forced Kurumbas to move to the edges of the forest, where they made a livelihood from selling forest produce and working as daily wage labourers for the Badaga farmers. They are still shunned, feared, and discriminated against for their old practices.

Tribes in Nilgiris have always been linked to one another by hereditary occupations, that formed the basis for exchanges and interactions between tribal communities. The Todas provide other tribes with dairy food, the Badagas with grain, the Kotas with craftware, and the Kurumbas with forest produce. Traditionally, they did not provide one another with labour or engage in market transactions. Anthony R. Walker, an anthropologist observes that 'economic exchange had ritual and social dimensions and took place not randomly in a market place but according to established relationships, mostly between families.' But the tribes never visited each other's villages.[17]

Even today, each Badaga commune has its own Kurumba 'watchman', which is a hereditary position. The watchman guards the village against supernatural danger. He also plays a necessary role in Badaga ritual, as an accessory to their priest. The Kurumbas conduct pujas for timely and plentiful rains, and when they cut the first furrows with a plough and sow the first seeds in the fields.

On the day of sowing, the Badagas set up a stone and paint it. The colours used are red and white made from soils, black from the bark of the kari maran tree, and green from the leaves of the kaatavarai sedi plant. The stone is also decorated with wildflowers. Sometimes, a goat is sacrificed as well. At night, the Kurumba watchman takes his lantern to the Badaga fields and performs panti odi, or garden sorcery, to give magical protection to the fields

---

[17] Bird-David, N. 'The Nilgiri Tribal Systems: A View From Below'. *Modern Asian Studies*, Vol 28 , Issue 2. 1994

and drive away elephants and pigs. Elephants are a big nuisance, trampling over water pipes and backyards. When a Kurumba sees a wayward elephant, he chants under his breath as he runs towards it with a burning bamboo torch. Elephants, they say, never fail to take flight. But whether it is darkness, spirits, or wild animals, Kurumbas fear nothing and no one.

In 1901, when Edgar Thurston, a British indologist, first conducted a study on Kurumbas, he found the term Alu Kurumbas missing in the Nilgiris. It seems to have been a development, perhaps from the late 1800s. Alu in Kannada implies milk, implying something good and harmless like milk. It is quite possible that to clear out or impair the negative opinion of them by mainstream society, a particular section of Kurumbas added the prefix 'alu' to their general identity. But to this day, there is minimal transaction among the tribes and each fiercely maintains its identity.

Even today, Kurumbas continue to act as healers by curing ailments, especially piles, joint pain and even diabetes. Flowers, roots, barks, twigs, climbing tendrils, twining shrubs and seeds are mixed with jaggery, breast milk, small onions, pepper, turmeric, and oils for application or consumption. Over time, however, this knowledge—passed orally from generation to generation— has diluted, as have the stocks of resources, as the Kurumbas moved away to the edges of the forest.

However, there are numerous treatments that are still in daily use. 'There's a root we use to cure piles. I can show it to you,' one Kurumba told me after retrieving the root from his stockpile. 'Look at the seeds. They have no name. They cure lack of desire in men,' another man showed his collection.

The Kurumbas refuse to reveal the names of plants and herbs used in their remedies because they believe that such revelation reduces their potency and invites supernatural punishment. The composition of each medicine is a closely guarded secret, passed only to one member of the family on the deathbed of the Kurumba healer. Often, knowledge of these medicines is also intuitive.

Kurumbas generally live in small nuclear families close to each other. There is no formal wedding ceremony; a couple is considered married when the woman starts living in the man's hut. Once the bride price (dowry given by the man's family to the woman's family) is paid off, the community starts recognizing the union. Kurumba children have only recently, since the start of the twenty-first century, started going to schools. They are frequently discriminated against and Badaga children refuse to sit with them. Eventually, discrimination and poverty force them to work in fields and forests.

Every spring, as the wind dies down and clusters of jacaranda flowers bloom on the shola trees, Kurumbas start following the bees in the forest—big, small or *nirjare*, the fly-like bees—as they collect sap from the flowers. The pollen sticks to the bees and falls off as they buzz back to the hive, creating a trail.

The Kurumbas follow these trails to be led to the hives. Given the geography of this part of the Nilgiris, the hives are often found on high, rocky cliffs. The Kurumbas mark the location with a bunch of leaves attached to a stick on the ground below the hive to let other Kurumba and Irula[18]

---

[18] Irulas, belonging to the scheduled tribe, are a Dravidian ethnic group in the Nilgiri mountains, in the states of Tamil Nadu and Kerala. They are known for their snake catching and honey hunting skills.

honey gatherers know that a claim to this hive has been staked. After scrutinizing the stage of development of the honey, they go away and return in summer to collect the mature honey.[19]

Kurumba men build tools for the task from scratch, including a wooden spear from a tall branch of a tree, a rope fashioned from a strong vine to be used for swinging against the face of the cliff, and a ladder made from cane and suryakodi plant. And then the panthai, a bunch of dried leaves of vazhaipul or banana flower, is used to smoke the beehive.

They climb the smooth cliffs, finding one improbable foothold after another. Sometimes snakes lodge near the hives, making it difficult to touch them. But a Kurumba swiftly pulls out a bugiri, a flute-like instrument, after smoking the beehive and plays it and then sings prayers, imploring the gods to listen to his call for honey. Within minutes, a keelback snake slithers out, as if disturbed by the incessant chanting. The honey collector then smokes the hive. A dark cloud of bees fly out, buzzing furiously at being drugged by the smoke. The bees escape into the bushes or fall to the ground. The honey collector slices the honeycomb with his spear and transfers the oozing honey into a basket tied to the end of the rope.

Kurumbas are said to be untroubled by bee stings as, over centuries, they have developed genetic immunity. On their way home, the honey collector and his mates munch on the honeycomb from the baskets dripping with honey,

---

[19] The period it takes for the honey to mature is known as ittu, or roughly speaking, from shirkarai to yani, in Tamil months.

making their chins and fingers sticky. They leave some of the honeycombs for the forest bears and squirrels.

In the evenings, they sit by the fire and play drums or crack riddles among themselves.

Ra du manegu ondu kambu. Adu e na ?

(Rough translation: 'One post for two houses. What's that? That's the nose.')[20]

Because of the forest's resources, food was never an issue for Kurumbas. In the cold weather, there was spinach on the slopes. In summers, there were jackfruits and mangoes. Their kitchen gardens took care of their supply of tomatoes, chillies and herbs. Berries, herbs, honey and tubers grew everywhere like weeds. This bounty meant Kurumbas never learned to farm because there was no need to grow and store food to survive.

While coffee plantations led to mindless deforestation starting in the 1830s, the forest laws also changed in the 1970s, reserving tracts of forest as biosphere reserves to protect the forests. Both had the same result—the Kurumbas lost their forests, whether it was when coffee planters expanded their estates or forest officials started driving them out.

Since the laws changed, the forest officials have falsely arrested the adivasis at the slightest pretext, confiscating their knives that they need to hack through the jungles.

---

[20] Kapp, Dieter B. 'Alu Kurumba Riddles', *Bulletin of the School of Oriental and African Studies*. 1984.

'Owing to the rigorous deforestation of the Nilgiri jungles during the past decades,' claims Dieter Kapp in his book on Alu Kurumaba[21], 'the tribespeople, who once lived fairly well on just what they cultivated in the fields and secured from the woods, have had to give up more and more of their ancestral living space and, consequently, have had to change their mode of life considerably. The end result is that the Alu Kurumbas have become impoverished and, in general, eke out a miserable existence today—a pitiable fact which shows, as in so many countries of the so-called Third World, that the "progress" slowly but surely causes the decay.'

Until the 1970s, the Kurumba honey collectors and medicine men used to make a living from selling honey, curing illnesses, and providing Badagas with incense, bamboo poles, resin and other religious products for the puja. Now, however, they earn a living by working in fields owned by others, which has changed forever the traditional life of freedom and of telling stories and singing songs.

Population: 4,874 Kurumbas (including all Kurumbas groups, in the Nilgiri district census, 2011)
Language: Kurumba language
Origin: Dravidians of south India

---

[21] Kapp, Dieter B. *Alu-Kurumba-Texte*. Otto Harrassowitz, 2006.

THE KHASIS
of Meghalaya

A peaceful matrilineal tribe that lives in urban spaces in deep harmony with nature.

Iewduh, Shillong's old market, is a honeycomb of lanes packed with shops. Each lane specializes in different things—masalas, pineapples, cane baskets, honey and pickles. Hawkers sit on the large stone steps in the grey smog, selling betel leaves and vegetables in wicker baskets, various parts of the pig and deliciously fried silkworms. Two or three women with sunburnt faces and cheekbones flushed like peaches mind these stalls, clad in the traditional garment called jainsem. Other female Khasi elders, called mei, walk through the passageways of the market, ordering men to pick up bags of produce.

Women predominate in this market space. Rural women begin gathering before dawn, when half the world is asleep, and carry on till their stocks are exhausted. Along with local Khasi tribespeople, there are also migrant communities who had set up shop decades ago. The market comes under the direct jurisdiction of the Syiem of Mylliem, the chief of the Vidhan Sabha. Every year, rituals are performed within the market areas, where there are big stone monoliths erected in memory of the tribe's ancestors and local heroes. This market is a living museum of women's culture and history in Meghalaya and beyond.

The Khasi tribals are said to have migrated from Cambodia about 66,000 years ago, along the plains of the Mekong River, which they regard as their 'elderly aunt'. They travelled through the Patkai Hills, through Assam, and settled in the hills and valleys of Meghalaya. Researchers found many monoliths, or stonehenge-like structures, in the Karbi Anglong district of Assam. These megaliths, similar to the monoliths in the Myanmar region, jut out sombrely against the sky. This leads anthropologists to conclude that the Khasis came in from around Cambodia, via Assam, before finally settling around Meghalaya.

Language is another clue to the Khasis' origin. Most of the other tribes who live in this region speak the Tibeto-Burman language. But the Khasi language is similar to the Palaung dialect dominant in Myanmar and the surrounding region.[22]

North east India has a unique geographic position. It is the only region that provides a land bridge between the Indian subcontinent and Southeast Asia. Many migrants and tribal societies came through the traditional route of migration from southeast Asia to the fertile valley of the Brahmaputra, through the Patkai Hills in the east, near today's Nagaland.[23]

[22] Cavalli-Sforza, L.L., Menozzi, P and Piazza, A., *The History and Geography of Human Genes,* Princeton University Press, 1994.
[23] B. Mohan Reddy, B.T. Langstieh, Vikrant Kumar and others, 'Austro-Asiatic Tribes of Northeast India Provide Hitherto Missing Genetic Link between South and Southeast Asia', *PLoS ONE.* 2007.

The Khasis are the most numerous tribe in Meghalaya. They are one of the last prevailing matrilineal societies in the world—a society where the wealth of the family is passed on to women, that is, from a mother to her daughter. Children receive their mothers' last names, and the youngest daughter—the *khadduh*—inherits the family's property. When she marries, her husband comes to live in her house. Even today, in an old-fashioned Khasi family, male babies are welcomed, but the birth of a girl calls for a feast.

Matrilineal Vs Martiarchal

Matrilineal denotes kinship with mother's side or the female line.

Matriarchal denotes a form or an organization where a woman is the head of society.

'Tang shu kha ka kime ka, ka kmie ka lah punkyrshah ia ka' (In rough translation, this means that when a mother dies, she passes on to her daughter the traditional festive checked apron called the *jain kyrshah*, leaving her responsibilities to the khadduh).

At a Khasi naming ceremony, a baby boy receives a sword, a bow, and three arrows to protect the family. A girl, on the other hand, receives the *ka khoh*, a basket, and a head strap meant for carrying loads in the cane baskets, symbolizing that women are meant to bear the burden of the family.

The khadduh is the head of the family and the custodian of the ancestral property. She has a duty to take care of her brothers, sisters and her mother's brothers, in case they return home after a divorce or are in extraordinary hardship.

For Khasis, god is present in nature—on the hills,
mountains, rivers, lakes, and forests. Large chunks of
forest have been preserved exactly as they have been
for centuries. To deprive a forest of trees, to Khasis, is
to refuse god his favourite space on earth. This gives
Khasi tribals a special impetus to maintain ancient sacred
groves called law-kyntang that are present all over the
Khasi and Jaintia Hills. They vary in size from a few
hectares to a few kilometres and are protected by local
communities as the sacred residences of local deities
and sites for religious and cultural rituals. They have
served as valuable storehouses of biodiversity for many
endangered plants like *Actinodaphne lawsonii, Hopea
ponga, Madhuca neriifolia* and *Syzygium zeylanicum*.

Mawphlang, in the East Khasi Hills district of
Meghalaya, near Shillong, is home to the most celebrated
of the law-kyntangs. The ancient Khasi Kyntang law
forbids the cutting of trees and any form of commercial
activity. Not even a single fruit, flower or leaf can be
taken out of the forest. As one enters this enchanted
patch of land in Mawphlang, the vegetation changes from
long pines to open mist-sprinkled grassland. Trees rise
like the columns of a giant cathedral into a thick canopy.
Underfoot is a thick carpet of crunchy leaves.

According to legend, the Mawphlang sacred grove grew from a
single sapling planted by a woman named Khmah Nongsai. Elders
of the Khasi clan had to perform a ceremony to request god for a
sign of their future ruler.

This forest harbours a diversity of flowering and medicinal plants, trees, mushrooms, birds and insects, and spans an area of seventy-eight acres. It is protected by members of the Lyngdoh clan and is believed to be the abode of the Khasi deity, Labasa.

The trees are wreathed by rare white, pink and violet orchids. Along the beaten path are bushes of box myrtle berries and echinacea flowers. Fallen jackfruits lie around, smelling overly sweet as they rot. Apart from rare plants, mushrooms and trees, the forest is also home to old coronation and sacrificial sites. This was where Khasi kings and ceremonial leaders (Ki Lyngdoh) had their meetings and new chiefs were anointed. The monoliths are along a slope, used decades ago for sacrifices of cocks and bulls, by the animist Khasis. Rhododendron flowers lie scattered around the monoliths. A wren-babbler bird lifts its head and whistles. Its mate picks up the strain and repeats it. A crested finchbill bird watches it all, unperturbed.

Animism Vs Pantheism

Animism claims that whether it is a tree or an animal or a human, every living thing has a soul and one can talk directly to the trees and ask for more fruit in the coming months.

Pantheism, on the other hand, states that all beings are one and that all actions are deeply connected to one another as a single being.

This forest, full of medicinal herbs, streams, and resource rich trees, has remained undisturbed for centuries now, in spite of being so close to urban centres. No Khasi indulges in wanton destruction, even where chopping trees is allowed. In the forests where logging is permitted, the woodcutter will do the job only after paying obeisance to god—who is the universe and manifests most closely through nature—through the ceremony of Ka Nguh ka Dem, where they bow in homage to the monoliths and trees, offering food and flowers.

The hills of Shillong are adorned by picturesque Khasi homes. Each home displays the characteristic love for nature—often with pots of beautiful flowers, especially orchids, lined up alongside. It is a common sight to see people watering their pots and sprinkling sugar for black ants crawling along the hedge. They nudge the mud around the flowers to add dry wood and coal powder to enrich the soil, moving with painstaking deliberateness. Collections of orchids are meticulously cared for, the leaves polished and the stems trimmed.

The traditional place of worship is the home of the khadduh. The clan gathers here to pray to ancestors to keep them away from pox, diarrhoea and even a smelly backside. An auspicious occasion calls for a ka-niam-ap, an elaborate feast to honour the dead, and to show respect for deceased ancestors with offerings. It is the responsibility of the khadduh to preside over these.

A little corner is created in the house with cane stools. These hold offerings of five betelnuts, five bananas, biscuits and rice, along with a pot of water, which are arranged around the urn that houses ancestral ashes. The tribe members gather around to chant and hum. A fowl could be sacrificed as part of the ritual. The offerings are kept out all night in case the ancestors want a midnight snack.

After the rituals, a wide array of food is served on cane mats—hot pots of nakhan bitchi or fish soup; tungtap or fermented sesame paste; and lots of pork—a favourite meat.

For members of the East India Company, the rituals of the gentle Khasis were shocking. The fact that they allegedly conducted animal and human sacrifices and ate meat ranging from bats to insects was an urgent reminder that they needed 'the blessings of the civilization' that Christianity would bring. A Baptist missionary, William Carey, went to this area in 1813 but was largely unsuccessful. Thomas Jones, a Welsh Christian missionary, who went to the Khasi Hills in 1841, was more successful as he involved himself with Khasi life, recorded the Khasi language in Roman script, and set up schools. By 1864, the British government had assumed almost the entire responsibility of educating the tribes. By 1866, there were some seventy schools in the hills, with about 1316 pupils.

Khasi opposition to the schools began when some pupils refused to join tribal rituals like animal sacrifice, praying to family spirits and eating raw meat. They cut their long hair and started covering their bodies, which contravened Khasi practices. Many of the women, however, were eager to learn since they felt it would aid in the many decisions that the matrilineal system placed in their hands.

Medical missionaries also helped in the rapid progress of evangelization. Khasis were often victims of outbreaks of cholera and smallpox. Before British intervention, the tribesmen resorted to sacrifices and local herbs or doctors from the Lyngdoh clan, traditionally the medicine men. The devastation caused by cholera was so severe that people started accepting foreign medicines and vaccinations. By the 1870s, Khasis ceased to regard Christianity as taboo. Today, about eighty per cent Khasis are Christians.

By the 1940s, with World War II, Shillong became the bustling convalescence base for Allied soldiers on the Burma front. With soldiers, came Willey jeeps, guns, dances at the Shillong Club, and western cinema halls. Young boys and girls swooned over the live concerts of Dame Vera Lynn, an English singer, who came to perform for the troops in 1944. Traditional instruments that were used during religious dances, like the duitara, a two-stringed musical instrument, and the tangmuri, a double-reed conical-bore wind instrument, became less popular than western ones.

The sacred groves and pools, traditional dances and festivals became less central to daily life. The dead were buried instead of being cremated and the ancient *mawbynas* or memorial stones, were flattened. In their place came new houses, markets and churches. The traditional among the Khasis were outraged at this deviation from age-old practices.

As a remedial measure, the Seng Khasi organization was formed in 1899 to counteract British and non-tribal influences. Elders renewed the emphasis for young Khasis to participate in traditional festivals, such as the Shad Shuk Mynsiem festival, which celebrates the arrival of spring but also reinstates their faith in the Khasi philosophy of the matrilineal system.

At this festival, every spring, girls wear the traditional rupa (armlet), sai khyllong (hair ornament), pansgiant (silver crown) with a lasubon (a silver attachment with flowers for the hair). The silver crown on each girl's head honours the position of women as keepers of the Khasi race. Men dance with whips and swords, in the role of protectors. In the inner circle, girls dance barefoot, eyes cast downwards.

Traditional Khasi social life is focused on the clan, with gatherings at the houses of the khadduh or other clan members. Vacations are spent visiting one another. The Khasi aunts would together slice vegetables for pickling, and later, sit with red tea and balls of fried rice dipped in jaggery as they gossiped. The conversations often flow this way:

'Iewduh seems to be getting smaller for our stalls,' one aunt usually complains. 'Have you heard Shylla is about to get married to a Christian?' Another would gossip about a distant cousin.

There has always been a concerted effort to keep young female members of the clan away from outsiders, especially non-tribal men. 'Don't hold their hands, or you may become pregnant,' they would warn. 'When you see them, walk in a cross pattern in your dhara to ward off trouble.'

There is also a rift between Khasis who practise the traditional religion and those who practise Christianity. 'Christians need saints to talk to Gods. For us, all we need are mothers and uncles—the priest and priestess. But the girls today . . .' one of the aunts would say while the others shook their heads. 'The Christians think they are superior to the indigenous Khasis. Face to face, they are polite, they sell us goods and sometimes eat at our tables—then turn around to bray and snicker about our rituals behind our backs,' another would complain.

The Christian Khasis, meanwhile, complain about the non-tribals, such as the Bengalis, Marwaris and Assamese, who have come to live in the hills, taking away their jobs. Moreover, this issue has led to many disputes, where the shops were burnt and the market was closed for days on end. Every time Iewduh (the market) suffers, all the hawkers suffer, whether tribal or non-tribal.

The youngest daughter in a family is recognized as the family priestess, and the oldest maternal uncle is supposed to be the spiritual and moral guide for his sister's children. Although women are the inheritors of ancestral property and gold, they do not possess the authority to buy or sell it without the approval and signature of the uncle.

Some Khasi women see their rights more as burdensome duties, while the men have fewer responsibilities. A woman can never be sure if the husband has more loyalty towards her and his children than towards his sister and her children, to whom he is the kni (guardian-uncle).

> Despite the three principal communities of Meghalaya—Garo, Khasi and Jaintia—being matrilineal in nature, traditional village bodies did not allow women to take part in the elections of heads for traditional village bodies, until 2020. Khasi society may be matrilineal, but it is not matriarchal.

As more and more Khasis move to nuclear set-ups away from their large, close-knit clan, matriliny places the burden of such societies on the mother. 'According to the matrilineal tradition, men aren't obliged to care for their children when they leave. This has led to a surge in women-headed households,'[24] which have only grandmothers, mothers and daughters. Many men are comfortable with leaving their families or drowning themselves in opiates. Some find matriliny against the principles of gender equality, as men do not inherit any property, nor do children get their names. The feeling of insecurity, typically borne by women in societies where the wife moves to the husband's home after marriage, is found among many Khasi men. Increasingly, as members move away from tribal practices, some Khasi men are now heads of their households, owing to their salaried incomes.

But nowhere else in India would you see so many women taking charge as they do in Meghalaya—whether it is at the vegetable shops, food stalls, government offices or private offices. Matriliny, so deeply entrenched in the fabric of their society, despite modernization, still persists.

Population: 1,427,000 (2011 Census of India)
Language: Khasi
Origin: Sino-Tibetan-Burman

---

[24] Rathnayake, Zinara. 'Khasis: India's Indigenous Matrilineal Society'. *BBC online.* 30 March 2021.

THE HILL MARIAS
of Chhattisgarh

A tribe which fulfils all the traditional notions of primitive innocence and an idyllic life, now battered by the demands of modernity.

The Hill Maria villages are located hours away on kutcha roads, within the deep forests of the Abujmarh Hills, in the Bastar region within Chattisgarh. These dense forests of Abujmarh have historically been isolated from the outside world from time immemorial, and accessible only via forest pathways from Narayanpur and other towns. During British rule in India, the Marias living in Abujmarh, known as Hill Marias, remained constitutionally excluded. This meant they were not part of their geographical maps, or subject to taxes or beneficiaries of any government scheme.

The forests have so much to give that the Marias have historically never felt the need to venture out. The seed pods of precious chironji (used in cooking) are carefully collected. Each opens to reveal a single seed, which is turned into a much-loved sweet pudding. Villagers scrap matured lac resin from kusum, ber and palash, a natural adhesive. The sal leaves, seeds, flowers, resin, and even the bark have medicinal uses in the treatment of leprosy, ulcers and diarrhoea. The leaves are used for cooking, preparing rice cakes, or smoking in pipes. The distilled leaves produce oil which is used in perfumes and for flavouring chewing gum and tobacco. The oil that comes out of its seed is known as sal butter and is used in cooking, burning oil lamps and sold to traders who use it for, if it must be told, adulterating ghee!

So important is this omnipresent tree that an adivasi marriage cannot be solemnised without its leaves. Every Maria wedding invitation has folded sal leaves, with turmeric and rice inside it.

In spring, the Marias lug the juicy fruits of the mahua and salphi (a regional variety of the palm tree). At dusk, boys camp in groves with fried chicken and spicy red chutney, made from ginger, garlic, red chillies, red ants, and ant eggs crushed together. After a short ceremony, they go from palm to palm, slit the barks, and collect the frothing liquid in leaf cups to drink. In a joyful state of semi-intoxication, they dance from village to village.

Men and women spend hours amassing their forest bounty, with breaks in between, to munch on purple jamun berries, take a dip in cool ponds or collect fish from them. They seldom travel beyond the market towns around the hills, where they trade the excess agricultural produce and forest goods for things like biscuits, talcum powder, and clothes. Although many Marias have now adopted mainstream professions and become doctors and teachers, most still live largely unaffected by civilization. Largely isolated from the outside world, their villages in the forests of Bastar are mostly inhabited by them and other sub-Gond tribes like Murias and Halbas. And within these forest precincts, they nurture age-old traditions and customs.

Men and women work in their fields, practising slash and burn agriculture. By evening, the older men and women sit under sal trees, exchanging news, weighing upon work done in the fields. When they exhaust all these topics, they open a bottle of mahua, made from the freshly fallen flowers of mahua trees. Every man has something to say about the mahua he's once had in Kondagoan or in the village of Babu Kohaka, or reminisce about the mahua that was had in a death or birth ceremony, at a festival, or offered by their son-in-law's family. They describe its floral scent and sharpness and recite songs and litanies in its honour.

Every child in Bastar is told the legend of the heroic Lingo, the youngest of seven brothers and a musician, who refused to succumb to the lusty advances of his six sisters-in-law, much to the relief of his brothers. His attention was wholly absorbed by a little hut outside the village, which he had built for himself. Its walls were made of fish scales, and its roof was made of snakes, and peacock feathers. Lingo played his eighteen musical instruments every night in this secret hideaway. Hearing the melodies, the young boys and girls would creep up to his hut by night and go back to their parents' home only after dawn. The reason, Marias say, that Lingo did not allow himself to be seduced, was because he was busy with the ghotul at his home, not only by its erotic delights, but also by its songs, dances, discipline and fellowship, with a peculiar mixture of restraint and freedom in relationships between the sexes. In a way, Lingo was the originator of the ghotul, and since that time, adolescent Marias finish their work in fields, forests and homes and wind up at their village ghotul.

Every evening, as dusk sets in, the usir bird sings, bringing with it joyous tidings. The adolescent and unmarried boys and girls head to their village ghotul, which is like a clubhouse. The boys usually arrive early to practise madri, nissan and pitorka gongs around a firepit. The girls have to finish household tasks, such as anointing the floor with fresh cow dung, husking the grain or cooking with their mothers. They dress up in their prettiest sarees, put on lipstick and powder, and hurry down to join the boys, sitting on logs placed beside the firepit at the ghotul. They crush dried tobacco, weeding out the moist leaves. Gossip and cowrie games are soon followed by wilder games.

Sometimes, they practise dance and songs for festivals. 'To the rhythmic lilt of a Gondi chorus, the children dance around the fire pits. The favourite dance is a rippling step forward with the foot dragged, singing "re-la", "re-la". In some villages, where the headman is an enthusiast, a trained band performs unusual and wonderful step dances to the sound of the drum.'[25]

This children's republic has the village panchayat as its ultimate head. Boys and girls choose their own leaders, called belosa and siredar, respectively. The boys oversee repairing roofs and fences while the girls sanitize the floor with cow dung and clean up ashes from the previous night. Both boys and girls have to clean themselves, oil their hair and dress in their finest attires to be presentable for the evening at the ghotul.

---

[25] Chandrapur District Gazette, Government of India, NIC, 1973

The Maria ghotul is also a centre for stern discipline. If there are transgressions, children may be asked to stand on one leg for hours or be whipped on their backs. Boys sleep in the ghotul every night, but girls usually return home in most villages.

A Maria Gond girl has the freedom to have premarital sex and choose a husband. As a married woman, she has the freedom to divorce if her husband ill treats her or if she cannot beget a child from him. She has the right to spend her earnings. A husband does not interfere in her affairs. However, women are considered taboo during menstruation, during which time they are not allowed to attend festivals. [26]

There is a level of physical and sexual freedom considered acceptable, which is unusual for mainstream India. Girls usually massage the boys or comb their hair, rubbing their arms and legs. In theory, it is the girls who choose their partners. In practice, boys often reject girls as a form of bravado expected from them by other boys in the ghotul. But if the girl rejects too many partners, it can result in a fine for misbehavior. A partner can also not sleep with the same person after three nights. The ghotul, as a community, has the responsibility of preventing unwanted pregnancies by avoiding sleeping with partners on specific days and avoiding emotional attachments.

Boys and girls spend time together in the ghotul for years. It is considered a mixture of learning and experimentation, none of which is meant to be taken too seriously. The boys stick feathers and play the drum; not to please any specific lover but to excite and gratify the

[26] Elwin, Verrier. *The Tribal World of Verrier Elwin: An Autobiography*. New Delhi: Oxford University Press, 1964.

entire ghotul. They fall in and out of love, are coveted by other partners, arrange to meet girls in forests, and play, sing and dance in the ghotul.

Every spring, when harvests are complete, the tribes look forward to the festival of cherchera punia. The boys and girls of each ghotul, dance and sing with members of the ghotul in other Maria villages. Hosts and visitors entertain each other with song and dance, sleeping in the ghotul for the night. In the morning, dancers wear their masks, go around the village, and stand before homes asking for auspicious liquor, rice, and pulses before returning to their homes—'Mai kothi ke dhan la harhera . . . ' (which roughly translates as 'Mother, please give the grains quickly.')

The Government of India has granted a concession to Adivasi tribals to manufacture, exchange and possess locally manufactured liquor for local consumption upon obtaining toddy licences for a period of one year. This privilege is given to the people of this community as they have been drinking toddy as an important part of their food and culture for generations.

The ghotul is much more than a place of entertainment. The peer group is obliged to provide services for weddings and deaths, as well as for road repairs and other odd jobs. When someone dies, Maria boys dig graves in their fields close to streams (unless a person has died of 'witchcraft', in which case, he should be burnt). They feed the grave with mahua (as an offering), while girls cook feasts, make flags for the grave, and dance.

The custom of making dead pillars, called 'gudi' in the local language, in Maria and Muria tribes is prevalent in south Bastar. Earlier, these could be wide, sharp and up to seven feet. The large stones were sliced from the rocky hills and carried down by the young boys of ghotul as well as the men of the tribe.

For happier occasions, like weddings, the ghotul children dress up in their finest beads and plume head gears. They dance in a circle and drink salphi, a form of alcoholic beverage derived from palm trees. Wedding preparations start almost a week in advance. The ghotul boys hunt meat and erect tents while the girls make leaf cups and plates. The bride and groom are slathered with turmeric, and given a bath by the girls while the boys fan them. The bride's combs—a sign of youth, mostly made and gifted to her over the years by the ghotul boys are removed and a farewell ceremony is performed for them—with coconuts, betelnuts and flowers.

'This will be your home until tonight', they sing.
'It was filled with your presence.
But now the house is silent.
You came here at the sunset
In your hand a broom
You went to clean ashes at the ghotul
Like a peacock dancing
You had a boy love
But now, you leave him behind sad and alone
You are going away

You were living in a kingdom of unmarried
You will never enter it again.'

However, things aren't always rosy in the ghotul. Life
for young people is full of hard manual labour—working
in fields, deboning fish, collecting logs, and caring for
younger siblings while parents work. For some, the life of
sexual freedom is not what they really desire. Some young
Marias eagerly welcome marriage, which they perceive as
a more 'permanent' relationship, with a stronger sense
of domestic morality, conjugal fidelity and stability than
the temporary relationships of the ghotul. Spouses are
mostly chosen by parents. There are very few recorded
cases of divorce.

Adivasi communities often have organized systems
for all community-related work ranging from weddings
and funerals to working in fields and medical crises.
According to Maria custom, on every important occasion,
the family ancestral spirits are called—to protect a
newborn child, make a marriage fertile, keep famine away,
ensure good rainfall, protect crops, or bring success in
hunting or fishing.

For medical complications, calling spirits and using
magical remedies and potions is common among Marias.
Gunias, the local doctors, have many herbal remedies
and chants ready. One can also seek out the sirhana,
the medium, who is believed to have the ability to call
and retain ancestral spirits within him, for solutions to
every problem.

If one were to head to a sirhana medium to pursue their love interests, he would, after long hours of chanting and drinking spirits, with his eyes rolling in the head claim, 'A strict meat diet of the virile organs of goat and ashes are to be offered to ancestors to pursue your love interest.' If nothing else works, he prescribes potent remedies like these—'Pursue a pair of sirhana cranes, for they always move in pairs. When one dies, the other quickly follows suit. Slip liquor down the throat of one of these birds, burn it and tie its vestiges around your waist. Your love interest will come running to you.'

Women do not have access to conventional medical help during childbirth, but death during labour is rare. When asked, a Maria woman responded to me, 'Now does the tigress need midwives for delivering her cubs?'

Until a few decades ago, life for Marias was generally peaceful and limited to the forest and its bounties. When outsiders discovered the rich resources of Bastar in the 1960-70s, they started mining in these regions. The government began taking away the lands of forest people and displacing them. Marias were paid generously for odd jobs like making roads and mining and provided alternative housing in other villages, in return for leaving their land. Even as they were pushed out of the forests, the Maria villagers were still dependent on the forests for medicinal herbs, grazing of their cattle, worshipping, burying their dead, fetching water for themselves and their cattle, collecting fuel and construction wood, among other things.[27] Over time, the overthrowing of their customary usage and access patterns and their traditional rights

---

[27] Deora, Shashank and Mahananda, Dhanamali. 'Forest Rights in Bastar: Of Tribals Being "Guests" in Their Own Woods'. *Down to Earth*. 5 November 2019.

started agitating them. Soon, the Naxalite movement also gained traction in the 1980s.

The Naxalites are far-left radical communists supportive of Maoist ideology. One of the underlying principles of the Naxal movement was the redistribution of agricultural land equally among all those engaged in agricultural production, particularly the landless.

The first Maoists arrived in the thickets of Bastar from the neighbouring states. Adivasis readily welcomed the armed insurgents demanding freedom for peasants and forest dwellers who were victims of mining laws and were fast losing access to the source of their livelihood—the forest.

The Maoists made their home in the 350,000 square miles of the jungles of Bastar, one of the last of India's unmapped territories. The CRPF and police set up camps everywhere the roads reached, but roads hardly reach anywhere in Bastar. For miles and miles, there are thick jungles and amidst their prowling cats (there are tigers in Bastar, but very few survive), the Naxals have charted their own paths and rules. Over the years, Bastar became infamously synonymous with the Naxalites who killed police with landmines and bombs and soon security forces retaliated with 'encounters'.

This has had a debilitating effect on the Marias as a tribe. Many are suspected of being government informers and punished within the tribe, or of being Naxal supporters and spending days in prison. As a result, many of them have now become guests in their own homes.

Population: Approx. 15,000-20,000 in Abujmarh Hills (Satellite Mapping, 2011)
Language: Gondi
Origin: Indigenous Dravidian

THE JARAWAS
of the Andamans

An ancient, isolated island tribe which has lived by itself for centuries and is now encountering modern civilization, often with disastrous effects.

In the azure waters of western parts of the South Andaman and Middle Andaman islands, sometimes, if you look closely at isolated corners of beaches beyond the forests, you might glimpse a Jarawa boy, sticking a rod into the shallow waters to hunt fish and turtles. Over centuries, the Jarawas have largely avoided interaction with people, apart from other tribes of the islands. Many details of their culture and traditions are still not well known.

The tribes of the Andaman Islands—the Jarawa, Great Andamanese, Onge and Sentinelese—are believed to have lived in their Indian Ocean home for over five millennia (50,000 years). Originally, it was believed to have been twelve tribes. Some anthropologists suggest that Jarawas migrated from Africa. Others suggest that they are descendants of early colonisers of Southeast Asia. Some believe Jarawas are descendants of the Jangil tribe, also of the Andamans which is now extinct. The Jarawas are both linguistically and culturally distinguished from the Greater

Andamanese tribes, of whom as a group, approximately fifty survive. Whatever their origins, the different tribes of the Andamans have lived in isolation from the rest of humankind for many thousands of years.

One of the earliest recorded reference comes from Marco Polo, who in his book, T*he Travels of Marco Polo* (c. 1300), gives an account of returning from China aboard a Mongol trade ship and describes the Andaman Islands as 'the land of the head-hunters'.[28]

In 1789, the Bengal Presidency of the British brought large numbers of people to these sparsely populated islands. There were several hostile encounters and hunts of the tribes and a major British attack in 1925 which killed many tribesmen. Like all the other tribes of the Andamans, the Jarawas died in large numbers due to the introduction of outside infectious diseases to which they had no immunity. The worst hit were the Greater Andamanese, hundreds of whom died in epidemics (pneumonia in 1868, measles in 1877 and influenza in 1896). Around this time, there was also immigration from India and Burma. During World War II, the tribes were even attacked by the Japanese forces. However, through all this, the Jarawas, like the other tribes, managed to survive.

After 1947, thousands of families displaced by Partition were sent to the Andaman islands. These families greatly feared the Jarawas, particularly on full-moon nights when Jarawas ventured outside their jungles, and into the settlements to loot fruit trees, granaries or even poultry. People would scurry home early, and those who couldn't

---

[28] Mazumder, Tanmay. *Andaman and Nicobar Islands*. Gurugram: Invincible Publishers, 2017.

reach home by nightfall would wait in government offices until the following morning.

In the 1970s, the Indian government decided to build the Great Andaman Trunk Road through the western forests. The road 'cut through the heart of their reserve forests and brought in busloads of refugee settlers into their areas.'[29]

As a result, the Jarawas not only encountered more possibilities for infection but also retaliated with some hostility at the enforced contact and to construction workers and loggers.

The Indian government sent several expeditions to woo the tribes, carrying coconuts, machetes, and bananas. But over time, officials unsettled the precarious Jarawa existence with gifts of alcohol and tobacco. Regular contact with outsiders also led to outbreaks of diseases like measles and pneumonia.

In April 1996, Enmei, a Jarawa boy with a foot injury, was left at a settler village and subsequently taken to hospital for treatment. During his five-month stay, he came into contact with many facets of modern life.

In October 1997, a boat full of Jarawas, including Enmei, made its way to Uttara Jetty in Baratung. It was the first time the Jarawas had voluntarily reached out to the settler population. Meetings with outsiders, especially with tourists, remained extremely dangerous to the Jarawas due to the risk of disease. But the Jarawas started to become regular visitors at settlements to trade, interact with tourists, learn other languages, get medical aid, and

---

[29] Bag, Shamik. 'Jarawa: Life on the edge'. *Live Mint*. 17 June 2007.

even send their children to school. A decade ago, most tribals spoke only the Jarawa language. Today, they mostly speak Hindi, but still hold onto the remnants of their ancient way of life.

Meanwhile, the Great Andaman Trunk Road became the route for what have been called human tourism tours. Even though the Supreme Court banned tourist traffic on this road in 2003, this order has never been enforced by the government. While the stated government policy is that 'no attempts to bring them (the Jarawa) to the mainstream against their conscience will be made' (2004), there is no unified attempt to implement it. There are distressing records of human tourism, where Jarawas are asked to dance naked for tourists in exchange for food, and many tales of sexual exploitation. A new development in the year 2022, proposes a plan to build a railway that cuts across the Jarawa territory.

Jarawas are pygmies, with most people under 145 cm in height. Neither men nor women cover their bodies. Interaction with mainstream life has exposed them to clothes, the threads from which are used to make ornaments, along with the more traditional shell, clay, leaves, flowers, and kangapo, or woollen threads. Many men decorate their bodies with white wavy clay patterns. Women use flowers, leaves and other parts of the plant.

Jarawas are said to have a very high health index among the aboriginals based in the Indian subcontinent as they eat fresh, raw and varied food. With bows and arrows, the Jarawa men hunt for pigs in the broad and open spaces within the jungle. When a pig is spotted, it is surrounded, and arrows are shot at it from as far as twenty metres.

They dig fish, including catfish-eel and pony fish, from shallow coral reefs and poke crabs from burrows in mudflats. The women collect turtle eggs, a delicacy among Jarawas, along with molluscs at the high water mark of the tidal flats. Caterpillars that fall from the canopy of the rainforest just before metamorphoses are also a delicacy. Women also gather tubers, seeds and seasonal fruits. A lot of animal meat is consumed, but Jarawas refrain from eating birds, which they fondly call 'noha'.

Forest herbs are used for medicines. Studies claim that Jarawas have botanical knowledge of about 350 animal species and around 150 plants. To cure cough and fever, leaves of *Amomum aculeatum* are placed on the chest. *Myristica andamanica* is used to stop bleeding. Betel leaf, especially piper betel, is used as a pain killer.

Honey is collected by both men as well as women. They set out on expeditions singing joyous songs. They chew on leaves such as Ooyekwalin and spread the sap around their mouths to keep the bees away. They cut and collect the hives in their straw buckets and hang them on their backs to head home. A ritual dip in the ponds or waterfalls always follows the messy affair of collecting honey.

Hunting involves complicated rules and rituals that involve elaborate praying before hunting with the community. The tribe has evolved and sophisticated tools which are hand carved. The bows and arrows are made of 'chooi' wood, for which they often travel far beyond the Jarawa territory. The harpoon arrow, known as tahowai khoab is made of areca wood, iron, and cane. The signature tool, the towa, is a knife used for cutting pork, made with much intricacy and fastened to the chest guards or kekkad. Women make fishing nets, baskets or taiga, and other tools for carrying food.

Though their territory is much more restricted, the Jarawas are still a nomadic tribe. When food seems scarce, they move from one place to another, to forage and socialize. Families visit relatives in other camps. Young boys of a camp-group often visit other groups to interact with their peer group.

During movement from one camp to another, men were observed to pack and carry their own hunting implements, while women carried food (honey, roots, tubers or smoked meat) in addition to their own belongings. Where there are crocodile infested creeks to cross, the Jarawas build temporary bridges with tree trunks. They tread carefully over slippery stones when walking through waterfalls and pause every now and then to rest with fruits and coconut water. Nowadays, they sometimes use the roads built by the government and hitch rides from lorries.

At a new camp site, the women and the children collect poles and leave to erect temporary shelters. Men go out in search of food. Young women erect their own shelter and make fires by rubbing stones to cook meat and heat water.

Each *chada*, a Jarawa hut, measures about a metre in height. It is usually occupied by a nuclear family of father, mother, and children from previous as well as current marriages. Once the children are around seven years old, they move out and live in bachelor or maiden huts. After this age, they move from one campsite to another independent of their parents. The young people live in same-gender groups (boys in thorkalang chadda and girls

in thorkongo chadda) until they get married. The widows
and widowers live with other widows and widowers.
During monsoons or in times of distress such as a tsunami,
the whole group lives together in one large community hut
with separate cooking hearths for each unit.

Both parents take care of the babies. Women breastfeed
not only their own babies but also those of their sisters
and other relatives when needed. Babies go everywhere
with their parents, tied to the father or mother with plant
fibre bands. Monitor lizard fat is used for massaging babies
because of its rich fat content. When the baby is weaned,
which is usually around one year of age, he is fed fish,
honey, and boar meat.

The coming-of-age ritual for boys is called lepa, which
is usually celebrated when a boy turns thirteen. The boy
goes on a wild pig hunt on his own, unlike the previous
occasions when he was accompanied by an adult. For a
girl, the coming-of-age ritual happens when she has her
first period. She is restricted to a small area in her house,
where she speaks to no one and her body is covered with
a mixture of alum, pig fat and gum. She sleeps on a bed
of deoa leaves, avoiding pig meat and honey, and eating
molluscs and water. After three days, she takes a long
bath and eats pig fat. When children attain puberty, they
are renamed, as it is believed that they have attained a
new identity.

For Jarawas, sex is an act to be celebrated and revered.
Young people spend long hours with their lovers in the
jungle without restrictions. Men and women woo each
other by eating monitor lizards, an aphrodisiac, and
smearing their fat on their bodies with clay. They make
designs on it with their nails, shells or wooden stencils

known as thomtangs. Pregnancies outside marriage are rare, because of the use of effective contraceptives like wachahi and hatho leaves. Marriages can be arranged by the couple themselves, or by their parents. In the latter case, the bride or groom often move to the same camp as the in-laws.

The Jarawas study the sun, moon, forest, and sea closely to ensure their safety and survival. The elements are carefully considered before taking any decision, including movement from one camp to another. They avoid travelling during the monsoons and at night. Moonlit nights are enjoyed with gegap (song) and paaloha (dancing). They can smell the wind. They can gauge the depth of the sea from the sound of their oars. So strong is their connection with nature that not a single Andaman tribal was killed by the tsunami of 2004, which killed approximately 225,000 people worldwide. The Jarawas claimed that they were warned by their ancestors through folklore and that they could forecast the weather. Therefore, they had occupied higher levels of the island hours before the waves hit the land.

Bartang, a town two hours from Port Blair, separates the forest reserves of the tribals from the settlers. It has become a big tourist spot, with active mud volcanoes, limestone caves, waterfalls and the biggest lure of them all—a chance of meeting with the Jarawas. Poachers and forest officials lure young tribal women with groceries, alcohol and meat for naked dances or sexually exploit them. Traditionally teetotallers, the men are offered foreign liquor in exchange for physical labour for making roads, felling trees, or taking forest resources like wood.

In 2003, when Enmei was visiting a hospital with his wife, a reporter asked him how he would react if his wife was exploited. He replied calmly, 'Nothing. She can take care of herself.' When asked if he wanted to move to the town, and be a part of the development, his response was, 'No, I'm happy in my jungle.'

While Harappa and Mohenjo Daro are celebrated all over the world and taught in schools, India's most ancient population, the Jarawas, who carry knowledge from more than 65,000 years ago are hardly mentioned in history and geography books. The Jarawas are perhaps the earliest freedom fighters who lived unto themselves, deep in these tropical woodlands, practically witnessing history before the arrival of British.

Today, the Jarawas are on the brink of extinction as settlers continue to occupy their lands and forests, cutting down their resources, and yet they refuse to give up their old lives, fiercely clinging to their roots and freedom.

Population: 380 (2011 Census of India)
Language: Jarawa / Gondi
Origin: Descendants of Jangil tribe from Andamans (who migrated to South Asia from Africa)

THE MEOS
of Rajasthan and Harayana

The Meos are a tribe based in north and north west Indian subcontinent, who played a significant role in the fight for independence and are a shining example of syncretism, following various rituals of both Hindu and Muslim traditions.

The Meos are a 400,000-strong community found in the region known as Mewat, which is spread across the border areas of the three states of Uttar Pradesh (mainly in the Chhata tehsil), Haryana (Nuh and Ferozepur tehsils of Gurgaon district) and Rajasthan, especially in Alwar district, where they have been able to preserve their unique culture.

If you drive across Alwar, you will see men in skull caps and women in bright ghagra-cholis. For hundreds of years now, this Meo tribe has practised both Hindu and Muslim rituals. They often have syncretic names like Lakshman Khan or Amar Khan or Fateh Singh, a product of different beliefs and various schools of thought.

Meo oral history traces their roots back to Mahabharat kings—the Pandus. While ancestral DNA tests, which chart genealogical descent, on the Meos revealed that their origins could be traced to the Indo-Scythians, a group of nomadic Iranian people of Scythian origin, based beyond the River Danube in Europe.[30]

How did a breakaway tribe of Indo-Scythians settle in these parts of India? They could be part of tribes such as the Saka Kings of Iran, who were 'horse riding' nomads who conquered and settled in parts of Pakistan and Afghanistan between 200 BCE–400 CE. Or they could have been pastoral migrators who moved while looking for greener pastures for their herds in the Middle East. They also could have been direct descendants of Alexander's army who ended up staying in India around 327 BCE to defend the occupied territories of Sind.

Sometime after the twelfth century, Meos started converting to Islam, which continued up to the sixteenth century. This shift could have been forced or influenced by Muslim rulers governing these regions, like Ghiyas ud din Balban (1216–1287; of the Mamluk dynasty of Delhi), Timur (1336–1405; who invaded India in 1398) and Firuz Shah Tughlaq (1309–1388; of the Tughlaq dynasty of Delhi). The location of the Meo lands meant that they were a popular refuge for rulers who were trying to gain control over the subcontinent.

But most of all, this shift could be attributed to a set of rulers called the Khanzadas, a community of Muslim Rajputs who established their chiefdom in the thirteenth

---

[30] Chawla, Abhay. 'How Meos Shape Their Identity'. *Economic and Political Weekly*. 5 March 2016.

century, near Kotla. Followers of Tablighi Islam,[31] Khanzadas constructed forty-one mosques, Islamic schools and tombs in the towns and villages of the Alwar region. Qazis were appointed to implement and govern with Islamic law ensuring marriages only to Muslims and ritual practices such as prayers and fasts. These Islamic laws must have also affected the social life of the Meos who participated in Islamic festivals and celebrated saints of Sufism, simultaneously celebrating Hindu festivals and traditions.

Babur (1483–1530), the first Mughal king, invaded this region in 1525. The brave and feisty Meos eagerly defended their lands but in vain. Pushed into the forestland, Meos took refuge in the sparse forests, depending on forest produce while hiding behind the brambles and bushes. The displaced Meos often resorted to looting and plundering in neighbouring villages for survival.

During the rule of Mughal emperor Akbar (1542–1605) in the next century, the regime slowly started hiring the displaced Meos as servants, spies and palace guards or the dak meoras and khidmattiyas. Due to their close association with the palace, the Meos were drawn further into the ambit of Islamic culture. Gradually, they started following nikah ceremonies with qazis in tow, burying their dead and celebrating festivals like Shab-e-Barat and fasting during the month of Ramadan. Sufi saint Khwaja Moinuddin Chisti developed a following among the Meos, who even today, visit his tomb regularly along with other Hindu and Muslim visitors.

---

[31] Tabligh is an Arabic word that means to reach out. To make Islam's message known to people is called tabligh.

Over the centuries, the Meos practised a synthesis of religions and cultures. They celebrate Diwali and Holi with as much gusto and pomp as Eid and Muharram. They visit powerful Hindu deities like Current Balaji, an incarnation of Hanuman worshipped in Rajasthan, and Karni Mata, the tutelary deity of the Rajputs and Charans of northwestern India who is an incarnation of Durga.

The Meo wedding rituals, for example, are predominantly Hindu. A practice followed by Muslims all over the world, including in India, is patrilineal and matrilineal cousin marriages. However, this practice is not followed by the Meos. During weddings and other rituals, Meos do not practice segregation of men and women, like Muslims. Much like Hindus, their guests intermingle and dine in the same areas without 'purdah'. When a man dies, in the Meo tradition, unlike more mainstream Islamic traditions, a brother or cousin can marry the widow of the departed through a simple nikah ritual.

The men wear pagdis or turbans like Hindus and the women do not wear burqas. They generally wear salwar kameez or ghagra choli with a light veil over their heads. Meo society is still divided into *pals* and *gotras*, as in Hindus, with clear rules about intermarriage.

The Meos speak Mewati, a language that has no script and can be written in both Devanagari script, used by Hindus, and Persian-Arabic script, used by followers of Islam.

Meo poets have their own retelling of the epic Mahabharat, *Pandun ka kada*, in which the Meos trace their origins to Arjun. This version begins with

Gorakhnath, a fakir (a Muslim austere who begs for alms) who follows the Hindu ideal of foregoing family and luxuries for an ascetic life. Gorakhnath possesses magical abilities with which he gives Kunti and Gandhari, the mothers of Pandavas and Kauravas, some grains of barley to make their barren wombs fertile.

Meo poets begin such tales or songs with a routine tribute to the ustaad (teacher) and to god (Allah) who is pak and subhan (untainted and glorious), before moving on to pay respects to Goddess Bhawani!

A captivating tradition observed by Meos is the recording of their genealogy by Hindu pandits who are also known as jaggas. The jaggas keep an account of all lifecycle ceremonies such as births and deaths in each family, creating a rich genealogical database for this community that has little written history. The Mirasi community of traditional singers in northwestern India, who sing songs of illustrious people, has several tales about famous Meo men such as Dariya Khan, the Gurchari Mev Khan story, or Panch Pahar ki Ladai. Some of these records reveal that Meos fought against British rule in the eighteenth and nineteenth centuries.

The story of Gurchari Khan and his brother Mev is about two strong and handsome brothers—Gurchari and Mev. The Mirasi bards, in their narration of the epic, sing that the two brothers were challenged to shoot at each other in such a way that the bullets meet midway. The brothers accepted the challenge and in a heroic display, their bullets crashed into each other. In another incident, they killed a tiger that was supposed to be the then

Maharaja's target. In a story of their fighting the British rulers, which is recorded only in the oral tradition, they are said to have cut electrical wires and threatened to stop all the trains if their demands for complete freedom were not met. In this much loved narrative, the brothers displayed a sense of fearlessness, rebelling against despotic authorities. In Robin Hood style, the heroes in narratives by Mirasis steal from the rich and give to the poor.

Over the centuries, under both Mughal and British rule, with the homes and lands of Meos being overtaken by invaders in various parts of their history, they were subjected to irregular taxes and revenue, while also suffering constant inroads into their independence. With the little documented evidence of tribes' lives, they often took to looting and rebelling and were reduced to petty criminals.

The Meos, however, perceived themselves very differently. A Meo calls himself the 'son of this soil' for defending India's independence at various junctures in the history of the freedom struggle. From Ghiyas ud din Balban, the sultan of Delhi in the twelfth century, to the British, they have challenged every invader. In 1857, during India's first war of Independence, more than 6,000 Meos sacrificed their lives fighting in dhars (organised mobs) with their Hindu brothers. Under the leadership of Siraj Sader-ud-din, a Meo farmer, they fought not only the East India Company but also British loyalist kings such as Alwar, Bharatpur and Jaipur, including their erstwhile Muslim brothers—The Khanzadas of Nuh. They not only managed to get rid of the East India Company from the

Mewat area of Haryana but also loosened the grip of the
East India Company in the Mewat areas under Alwar and
Bharatpur states.

For years, the Meo community has had rich
relationships with Jats and Gujjars. They live intermittently
across the once-contiguous belt of Rajasthan, Uttar
Pradesh and Haryana, and there is mutual respect for
religious choices and rituals.

In 1926, Muhammad Ilyas al-Kandhlawi established
the Tablighi Jama'at in Mewat, a city that is home to
many Meos. It grew to become a transnational Deobandi
Islamic missionary movement that exhorts Muslims to
be more religiously observant by practising the religion
as preached by the last Muslim prophet—Muhammad
Ibn Abdullah. Jamats began promoting their idea of
what being a Muslim meant. Riots between Hindus and
Muslims broke out in the Mewati region in the run-up
to Independence in 1947. Towards the end of the British
rule, with independence looming on the horizon and
the hardening of communal forces, there was a mass
migration of Meos to Pakistan, while others camped
around Punjab, resisting the urge to leave their beloved
land. The riots led to mass deaths, leaving a shadow of
the Holocaust in the region.

Many Meos were routed or murdered by mobs, who
came from various strata of society, in the riots preceding
independence. The Meo villages were burnt to the ground,
and those allowed to stay were subject to purification or
conversion back to Hinduism.

In December 1947, Gandhi visited Ghasera village to urge the Muslims living there not to leave the land of their forefathers for Pakistan. He said that the Meos were the 'backbone of India' and would never be forced to leave its soil. He managed to ensure a large population around Delhi was not forced to leave.

On 30 January 1948, Gandhi was assassinated, shaking the Meo belief but many stayed back. Mewati Divas, to commemorate Gandhi's visit, is celebrated every year.

After many Meos embraced the infamous Tablighi Jama'at's version of Islam in 1926, the Tablighi Jama'at re-socialised this community, which once followed both Hindu and Islamic rituals, into the pure Islamic fold.

Soon after, the jaggas and Mirasis felt pressured to give up their age-old associations with the tribe.

In recent times, the Meos have been in the news since Pehlu Khan from Alwar (also in Mewat) was allegedly lynched by a mob in 2017 while transporting cows for his dairy farm. Soon after the murder, the Meos called for a ban on cow slaughter and for the cow to be declared India's national animal. Underlying the ban, however, is an unusual religious-cultural identity that manifests itself in a combination of 'cow worship' and offering namaaz in the community.

So, what are the Meos then, Hindus or Muslims? Try insulting the Pandavas of Mahabharat, whom the Meo consider their original ancestors, and see their anger and revulsion. Understanding Meos and their various rituals forces us to realize that perhaps our definition and imposed boundaries of culture and identity are profane and gives rise to a crucial question—why should a person be limited to the practices of just one religion?

Population: 1,70,000
Language: Mewati
Origin: Hindu Meena and Rajput clans, who converted to Islam between the twelfth and seventeenth centuries

THE BHILS
of Rajasthan and Gujarat

A tribe with a formerly glorious history of kingship which is now struggling to adjust to the modern world.

In the Mahabharata, Eklavya is a Bhil boy whom Dronacharya refuses to train because the former's unsurpassable skills with bow and arrow are a threat to the supremacy of the latter's most accomplished student—Arjun. Dronacharya asks Ekalavya where he acquired his archery skills. Ekalavya responds, 'Under you, Guruji.' To ensure that Arjun would be the best archer in the world, Dronacharya asks Eklavya for his right thumb as a form of 'guru dakshina'. Aware that he would never be able to shoot an arrow again, Eklavya complies.

The name Bhil is derived from the word 'billu', which in Dravidian languages implies a bow. Till today, the Bhil tribe take pride in the traditional craft of making bows and arrows with bamboo, cane, iron, rope, and feathers. It is said that Bhils can strike a target from a kilometre away. Although hunting is officially banned under the provisions of the Wild Life (Protection) Act 1972, Bhils remain hunter-gatherers. They usually hunt at night, to avoid forest officials. The game is brought home for feasts and celebrations, much to the horror of their neighbouring tribe—Bishnois. Bhils often live in the same areas as Bishnois, who do not eat meat, or fell trees and follow strict rituals of purity around villages in Madhya Pradesh, Rajasthan, Gujarat, Chattisgarh and Maharashtra.[32]

The Bishnois are followers of Guru Jambheshwar (1451–1536), the founder of the Bishnoi Panth who taught that god is a divine power that is everywhere.

In 1730, the Maharajah of Jodhpur wanted to build a new palace. He sent soldiers to gather wood from the forest near the village of Khejarli, near Jodhpur, where Bishnois had grown an abundance of khejri or acacia trees. When the king's men began to cut the trees, a Bishnoi woman, Amrita Devi decided to hug a tree and encouraged others to do likewise. As villagers each hugged a tree, they were beheaded by the soldiers. About 363 Bishnoi lives were sacrificed. Upon hearing of this, the king rushed to the village and ordered the soldiers to cease. He designated the erstwhile Bishnoi state in western Rajasthan a protected area. This legislation still exists today in the region.[32]

There are several origin stories of the Bhils. One of the most popular is that one day Lord Shiva was ill and resting in a rocky, dry and arid area of a forest. A beautiful woman appeared before him, a single glance from whom cured his illness. They had several children together, one of whom grew up to be bitter and vicious. He killed Shiva's ox and his angry father drove him to the forests as punishment. This boy lived in the forest, fed on wild fruits, and grew close to animals. His descendants were called Bhil. To this day, Bhils consider forests their home.

---

[32] Global Nonviolent Action database (nvdatabase.swarthmore.edu).

Many similar origin stories of the Bhils exist and most ascribe their origin to some wrongdoing, a tragedy, or an incestuous act. This automatically casts them as inferior or immoral human beings, and usually of lower lineage.

There are mentions of Bhil kings in the Mahabharatha, some historical texts and some that hover between mythology and history. Bhils are mentioned in the Mahabharata as rulers of Rajputana, Malwa, and some parts of central India, as well as territories in southern Gujarat. In 1400 BCE, it is said that one Krishna Raja defeated the Bhils in present-day Gujarat and established his kingdom there. At that time, the Bhil queen Doshra was allegedly the ruler of Malwa state comprising a large portion of the present-day western and central Madhya Pradesh, and parts of southeastern Rajasthan and northern Maharashtra, whose ancestors had ruled Malwa for 287 years.[33]

There are records of Karna (1064–1092 CE) of the Chalukya dynasty of Gujarat, killing the Bhil chief of Ashapalli to lay the foundations of modern-day Ahmedabad. In 1190, a Bhil king, Jetsi Bhil, lost his throne to king Bheemdev II of Gujarat, who had been refused his daughter's hand.

The Bhils and Rajputs have had a long history of conflict, though the former is celebrated in the writings and verses of the latter, for their bravery and heroism. Their long association is symbolised in the erstwhile Mewar royal signages, which show a rising sun flanked by a Rajput on one side and a Bhil warrior on the other. In the

---

[33] Singh, V.P. and Jadhav, Dinesh. Ethnobotany of Bhil Tribe. Jodhpur: Scientific Publications, 2011.

proud military history of Mewar, the Bhil tribesmen have played an important part.

Largely, Bhils could be identified as one of the Dravidian racial tribes of Western India, belonging to the Australoid group—denoting the broad division of humankind represented by the Australian Aboriginal group of tribes. They speak a language of Dravidian origin. Currently, India's most populous tribal group, they have been exploited for centuries under the British rule and later by the government of independent India. Uprooted from their ancestral lands by invaders and then the government, they quickly took to rebellion, being tagged as outlaws and criminals.

For most of their recorded history, however, the Bhils have maintained a distinctive social structure and mode of life. They have always lived in arid, uninhabited lands and have thus been separated from other people by geography. Historically, they belonged to no kingdom and were compelled to fend for themselves by looting during times of extreme scarcity, like the drought season. In this struggle for survival, they are reputed to have killed hundreds of people.

Some historical records suggest that Bhils were victims of the caste system and were criminalized by Rajput clans. They may have been landowners in Khandesh (present-day Maharashtra and Madhya Pradesh) but were forced into the forests by Rajput rulers in the sixteenth century, and later the Peshwas and Marathas in the eighteenth century.[34]

---

[34] Kushawaha, Subhash Chandra. *Bheel Vidroh: Sangharsh Ke Sawa Sau Saal*. New Delhi: Hind Yugm, 2021. (Hind Yugm, 2021).

There are numerous Bhil revolts against the various rulers who tried to oppress them—against the Peshwas (1804), local chieftains and kings, and later the British rulers. Some important heroes of Bhil rebellions include Nadir Singh Bhil (1802-1820), Gumani Nayak (1819-1820), Cheel Nayak, Dasharath and Kania revolt (1820), Hiriya Bhil (1822) and Bhari Bhil (1824). There are other stories of a historical battle in Nasik (1835) and Kunwar Jeeva Vasava in 1846.

All through the nineteenth century, the fiercely independent Bhils refused to come under the British yoke, who tried to make them pay taxes, hunt for officers or work as manual labourers. There were allegedly eighty notorious Bhil gangs with over five thousand followers. As a consequence, they were designated a criminal tribe like the Kanjars. This essentially meant that they could be 'randomly picked up, tortured, maimed or even killed'[35] by the colonial authorities.

In the late 1800s, the British discovered that cotton plantations around Maharashtra were a lucrative source of income. Seeing an opportunity, Gujjar tribes started coming back to these lands from Gujarat and Rajasthan, to become moneylenders or cultivators. They too began to exploit the Bhils, who had to pay taxes to the British and provide underpaid labour to Gujjars.

In 1913, under the leadership of Gobind Guru (1858–1931), a social and religious reformer, who demanded better working conditions, 1500 Bhils gathered at a British bastion, Mangarh Tekri on a hill in Dungarpur,

---

[35] Abraham, Susan. 'Steal or I'll Call You a Thief: "Criminal: Tribes of India'. *Economic and Political Weekly*. 3 July 1999.

southern Rajasthan. Suspecting a rebellion, the British troops opened fire and over a thousand were killed. This massacre is seldom written about in history books, further relegating the Bhils to obscurity in the history of the freedom struggle.

After repeated conquests by Hindu kings, the animism rituals that the Bhils followed—animal sacrifices, praying to trees and sun—were soon replaced by Hindu practices. Certain Hindu taboos became an integral part of the Bhil tradition. This is especially seen in the superstitious regard for a dead body, a new-born child, blood—particularly a woman's blood and therefore women in general because of the menstrual cycle.

In the adivasi heartland of central Gujarat, Madhya Pradesh and Rajasthan, the fear of 'dakan' holds sway over the unschooled and superstitious community. The Bhils believe that when an unnatural death occurs, a spirit enters the body and speaks or acts through it. The wicked souls particularly enjoy haunting women—notably, dakin (witch) and suril (churail). The locals, both Bhil and non-Bhil, say that the host woman loses control and gains extraordinary strength. Bhopas, the priests, host the good spirits that help in recalling the past, prophesying the future and curing ailments. In his dealings with the spirits, the Bhopa largely depends on coaxing the spirits while a witch uses coercion. Therefore, a witch is regarded as treacherous and vile. If a woman is to be found practising witchcraft or be plagued by it, she is either killed or exiled.

The locals believe that witches are mostly middle-aged or older women who take human or animal forms, especially cats or younger women. There are many superstitions concerning the attributes of a witch. Her eyes are said to glisten like those of a cat, and her powers are beyond those of a human. If one looks directly at a witch, one can be suspended upside down. Witches are said to greatly enjoy a person's liver. They can be quite belligerent if they take a liking to a person, snitching them away into the forests to make a meal out of them. A witch can be distinguished from other women by the look in her eyes, her wicked smile and her persistent behaviour. A woman whose mother is a witch or who has been breastfed by one also becomes a witch. The wrath of the locals falls upon the witch when a person experiences continuous ill health or disease.

A Bhil matriarch in Ambua, Rajasthan recalled her experience with a witch. Pointing to a hut, she spoke in Bhili, an Indo-Aryan language. 'See that hut, it belongs to Methu ki maa [Methu's mother],' she said. 'That dakin doesn't allow Jurusingh to eat a thing. And when the Bhopa tried to talk to the witch, she entered Jurusingh's body and wailed—"He refused me milk when I came to his hut as a cat, drank it himself and then kicked me. I will eat his liver and finish him within days."' Jurusingh apparently died a week later.

Families scheme with witch doctors to exact revenge or seize the property of women by branding them as dakans. These women are beaten, harassed, abandoned, heavily fined, or even put to death, though there is little record of numbers. Bhil villagers as well as the medicine-men are now afraid of pointing out witches, as it is forbidden by law and punishable by imprisonment. Cruelties of this kind have reduced considerably, but the belief in witchcraft is still omnipresent and strong.

Women are also excluded from most religious ceremonies. They are considered to have less aptitude and incapable of performing jobs that require elaborate measures. Unlike extravagant rituals conducted by men, Bhil women do short pujas with incense and coconut husks burnt on a plate, the smoke directed towards the goddess Kalika, the earth mother. They believe that they are *gandi* (impure). Women performing religious tasks is considered risky as it can make children and cattle sick.

There are people who argue that there is no drastic gender inequality among Bhils. Photographs of older Bhil women in koti-kanchli (the traditional outfit of Bhil women), wearing a variety of ornaments like hansli (necklace), rings, zele-zumke (earrings), narniyan (bangle), nathni (nose-jewel) and smoking *chillum* (smoke pipe) or hookah are cited as evidence of women's emancipation in the tribe. The fact that men pay a bride price to a woman's family is also cited as evidence of women's power.

The miserable truth is that the bride price is essentially used to 'buy' women. A virgin commands the highest price, as do young and beautiful women. The money received is used by the men of the girl's family for alcohol or other pleasures. A wife is considered a possession of the husband's family. In case the husband dies, she is married to her younger brother-in-law.

Polygyny, where men can have more than one bride, is prevalent among the Bhils. However, since brides have to be 'bought', men usually end up with just one. In the past, bride price was circumvented by kidnapping women. This was called gis len ayo, where a married woman is 'kidnapped' from her home. Some decades ago, it was estimated that almost one-fifth of all marriages were ones where the bride had been abducted, sometimes of her own accord. This resulted in massive feuds among villages when husbands discovered that they had been betrayed.

Each Bhil wife has to set up a home in her husband's village, near his father's homestead. Each wife, where there are multiple, is entitled to her own abode. They live in hive-like huts cresting the tops of isolated hills or faraway hamlets, away from non-tribe habitations. The senior wife is the one who divides labour among all, ensuring equitable distribution.

Today, most Bhils live in homes made of unburnt bricks and mud roofs. Traditional Bhil art adorns the clay walls. Bhil paintings usually consist of large, unlifelike shapes of everyday objects and characters, filled in with bright, earthy colours. The shapes are then covered with an overlay of uniform dots in several patterns and colours that stand out against the background. The dots on a Bhil painting are not random and have their own symbolism. The paintings are done with neem sticks, twigs, bunched-up cloth, and using natural dyes like turmeric, beetroot, flowers, vegetables, leaves and oil. The paintings on floors and walls portray life experiences—childbirth, a woman dancing to ghoomar to announce their stepping into womanhood, a day in the maize fields, or a woman making maize rotis on fire.

With a ban on hunting and access to forests, food is scarce in these desert regions and mouths are many. While their men, like most rural farmers in India, struggle to earn an income and find solace in local arrack, women now often migrate to bigger cities like Ahmedabad in search of daily labour.

India has one of the most well-preserved systems of a class-based society. In practice, that means that the Bhils are attempting to enter a society that regards them as inferior human beings as a matter of theoretical belief. Along with a lack of education, this means that Bhils only find jobs like those of domestic help and sweepers and drain cleaners with municipalities in bigger cities.

As modernizations threatens to relocate these tribal populations from their last fastness in the hills and forests, surprisingly, hardly any focus remains—be it from NGOs or the government—on restoring them to their homes. What the world refuses to realize is that tribal lives and lifestyles—a synthesis of the traditional and the modern— hold a promise of survival not only for them but for humanity as a whole.

Population: 16,00,000 (2011 Census)
Language: Bhili
Origin: Indo-Aryan

Nidhi Dugar Kundalia is a journalist and her stories and essays have appeared in various national newspapers and magazines. She mostly writes on socio-cultural issues, documenting human lives and their journeys through various settings. Her first book, *The Lost Generation: Chronicling India's Dying Professions,* was released in 2016 to a warm reception. Her second book is *White as Milk and Rice: Stories of India's Isolated Tribes*. She is a graduate of the School of Arts, City University, London and lives in Kolkata with her husband and children.